F9F PANTHER
VS
COMMUNIST AAA

Korea 1950–53

PETER E. DAVIES

OSPREY PUBLISHING
Bloomsbury Publishing Plc
Kemp House, Chawley Park, Cumnor Hill, Oxford, OX2 9PH, UK
29 Earlsfort Terrace, Dublin 2, Ireland
1385 Broadway, 5th Floor, New York, NY 10018, USA
E-mail; info@ospreypublishing.com
www.ospreypublishing.com

OSPREY is a trademark of Osprey Publishing Ltd

First published in Great Britain in 2022

ISBN: PB 9781472850645; eBook 9781472850638; ePDF 9781472850669;
XML 9781472850652

22 23 24 25 26   10 9 8 7 6 5 4 3 2 1

Edited by Tony Holmes
Cover artwork and battlescene by Gareth Hector
Three-views, cockpit views, Engaging the Enemy and armament scrap views
by Jim Laurier
Maps and formation diagrams by www.bounford.com
Index by Fionbar Lyons
Typeset by PDQ Digital Media Solutions, Bungay, UK
Printed and bound in India by Replika Press Private Ltd.

Osprey Publishing supports the Woodland Trust, the UK's leading woodland
conservation charity.

To find out more about our authors and books visit
www.ospreypublishing.com. Here you will find extracts, author interviews,
details of forthcoming events and the option to sign up for our newsletter.

F9F Panther cover art

On September 3, 1951 future astronaut Ens Neil Armstrong made his 28th
catapult launch from USS *Essex* (CV-9), heading for target area "Green Six" –
a narrow valley near Wonsan. Flying with USAF exchange officer Maj John
Carpenter, he dropped 500lb bombs on a freight yard and Type 92 7.7mm
and DShKM 1938 12.75mm machine gun positions around a bridge target.
There was heavy AAA opposition, resulting in an AD Skyraider being shot
down and Armstrong's F9F-2 being hit in a wing tank, causing the loss of
elevator control. Flying at more than 400mph at less than 500ft, Armstrong
failed to see a wire trap attached to poles running across the valley. The
resulting impact severed six feet from his starboard wing. Despite hydraulic
damage that made the flaps and landing gear extend, Armstrong managed to
nurse the Panther back at 170mph to safe territory near Pohang air base, using
his trim tabs as controls. He then ejected, subsequently landing in a
foul-smelling rice field. Returned to *Essex*, Armstrong flew again the following
day. (Cover artwork by Gareth Hector)

North Korean AAA cover art

A North Korean M1939 (52-K) 85mm AAA weapon emplaced near a bridge
close to Chando-ri fires at VF-831 F9F-2 Panthers on July 19, 1953. Other
camouflaged guns are positioned nearby on the riverbank, and troops with
light automatic weapons are also in place to defend the bridge. Attacks on this
type of target were flown throughout the war, and North Korean AAA
defenses were concentrated around them. (Cover artwork by Gareth Hector)

Previous page

A VF-72 F9F-2 flown by Lt R. P. Yeatman fires HVARs at a bridge in North
Korea in November 1952. Perforated dive brakes, deflected by up to 75
degrees for dive attacks, are extended below the forward fuselage, although
they caused a nose-down change in trim that could adversely affect the pilot's
aim. This aircraft is also armed with 250lb bombs, one of which can be seen
falling away beneath the rocket smoke. (CORBIS/Corbis via Getty Images)

CONTENTS

INTRODUCTION

A captured NKA 37mm gun, the scourge of F9Fs flying at low and medium altitudes. Behind it is a 40mm weapon with its barrel in the vertical position, and two 85mm guns can be seen on the horizon. The muzzle flash from a 37mm weapon was only clearly visible to pilots who were flying directly at one as the gunner fired a seven-shot clip of shells at them. (USAF)

Anti-aircraft artillery (AAA) evolved to match the numbers and capability of the aircraft it opposed. Germany entered World War I with just 18 anti-aircraft weapons, but by the end of the conflict its gunners had become sufficiently well-equipped to claim 1,588 United Nations (UN) aircraft destroyed, although they required an average of 5,000 rounds (reduced from 11,600 in 1915) to bring each one down. Searchlights, telescopic range finders, acoustic detecting devices and improved fuzes with mechanical timers were then added to the gunners' arsenal.

Development remained fairly static in the inter-war period, with 3in. calibre guns and acoustic detection still in place, despite dramatic improvements in aircraft performance. In the late 1930s, when much of the AAA used by communist forces in the Korean War was being designed, more powerful guns of around 90mm bore were advocated. Germany chose an 88mm Krupp-Bofors model for 60 percent of the country's standard heavy Flak weaponry during World War II. It remained in use with the Korea People's Army (KPA) into the early 1960s. The 88mm guns fired shells fitted with either contact or timed fuzes, although proximity fuzes (adopted by Allied forces during World War II) that could have made the weapons three times as efficient were not used by the KPA during the Korean War.

Radar-directed guns were not widely available until late 1944, and thousands of acoustic sensing devices remained in use. Britain chose to field 3.7in. AAA weapons, and pioneered gun-laying radar to

find and track targets for its batteries from October 1940.

Flak destroyed more US aircraft than any other weapon during World War II, particularly during the massive daylight bombing offensive against Germany that commenced in 1943. For low-flying tactical aircraft, it also became the main killer. AAA graduated from being a nuisance to determining the outcome of many air operations.

At the very least, it reduced the accuracy of many attacks by overloading pilots with threats as they attempted to concentrate on delivering their ordnance. Mission planners sought to avoid known AAA positions where possible, although this often meant prolonging routes and allowing for chaff and jammers to be carried by the bombers. Flak suppression missions, the most dangerous assignments for tactical aircraft, became necessary to reduce the threat.

The Korean War presented some unprecedented military situations for UN forces, although pilots faced all the well-established threats described above. There were few strategic targets, USAF units were denied land bases for several months, and UN forces were confronted by overwhelming Soviet and Chinese air and ground forces, as well as North Korean armies. US defense strategy was based on nuclear deterrence, but in Korea it had to respond to conventional communist aggression initially with surplus World War II armament and aircraft.

Communist ground-based air defenses were dated and, at first, spread thinly across the country, with concentrations in specific, avoidable areas. Although the number of AAA weapons in-theater increased significantly following China's entry into the war in October 1950, the total number of guns available by war's end was still fewer than German forces would have deployed to defend just a single city in 1945.

The US Navy had two new jet fighters, the McDonnell F2H Banshee and Grumman F9F Panther, to support its predominantly propeller-driven strike aircraft. In 1949, the dominance of the USAF's Strategic Air Command (SAC) and its huge demands for funding had caused inter-service battles in which the US Navy's flagship carrier, the 65,000-ton USS *United States* (CVA-58), was canceled just five days after its keel was laid. With it went plans for a new generation of naval strike and fighter aircraft that would have included swept-wing types to rival those entering USAF service.

Nevertheless, the straight-winged Panther and Banshee entered service in 1949, which meant that by the start of the Korean War in June 1950, the US Navy had its first combat jets embarked on board carriers. Their success in that conflict did much to revive the aircraft carriers' fortunes, and the first of the new generation of 75,000-ton *Forrestal*-class 'super carriers' was commissioned in 1955. The US Navy could then catch up with the USAF in developing another generation of jet fighter and attack aircraft.

An F9F-2 from VF-23 is hooked up to one of *Princeton*'s two catapults, ready for a quick launch should any potential aerial threat be picked up by the carrier's search radar. This squadron was CVG-19X's only Panther unit embarked in *Princeton* during the carrier air group's brief May 31 to August 29, 1951 combat cruise. (National Archives)

CHRONOLOGY

1941
June

The USSR enters World War II with the M1938 76.2mm and M1939 (52-K) 85mm heavy guns, the M1939 (61-K) 37mm medium gun, and DShKM 1938 12.7mm machine gun as its primary AA defenses.

September

Bell Aircraft Corporation receive a contract for three XP-59A Airacomet fighters, the first US jet aircraft, powered by license-built British Whittle W.2B engines.

1943
August

Following testing of the XP-59A, the US Navy awards the little-known McDonnell Aircraft Corporation a contract for the XFD-1 (later FH-1) Phantom jet fighter. It subsequently makes the US Navy's first carrier landing by a jet on January 21, 1946. A total of 66 aircraft equip one US Navy and two US Marine Corps squadrons from 1946.

1945
January

North American Aviation receive a contract for the XFJ-1 Fury jet fighter. Grumman's Design 71, an early version of the F9F concept, is rejected.

September

Grumman begins work on its XF9F-1 two-seat jet nightfighter.

1946
October

The XF9F-1 contract is replaced by one for the Design G79D (XF9F-2) single-seat fighter powered by a Rolls-Royce Nene engine.

1947
January

The XF9F-2/3 mock-up is approved.

November 21

The XF9F-2 prototype flies.

1948
August 16

The XF9F-3 (Allison engine) first flies.

1949
Spring

USSR introduces the KS-19 100mm AAA weapon into service.

May

F9F carrier suitability trials begin. VF-51 receives its first F9F-3s.

September

VF-51 becomes the first operational fleet squadron, embarked in USS *Boxer* (CV-21).

December 21

First flight of the XF9F-5. Deliveries begin in November 1950.

1950
April

VF-51 and VF-52, embarked in USS *Valley Forge* (CV-45), begin a Far East cruise.

June 25

The Korean War begins.

July

The F9F-4 first flies.

July 3

The first US Navy jet combat mission results in the first jet aerial victories (for VF-51) when *Valley Forge* F9Fs provide CAP for attacking Corsairs and Skyraiders and shoot down two North Korean People's Air Force (NKPAF) Yak-9s.

July

Gen Peng Dehuai asks Chairman Mao Zedong for two of his twelve AAA regiments to defend the bridges at Andong and Ji'an from the south side of the Yalu River.

Summer

S-60 57mm AAA weapon enters Soviet service.

August 12 F9F-3 BuNo 123068 from VF-51 becomes the first Panther to be shot down by communist AAA when it is hit while strafing a train north of Kumchon. The pilot, Ens John Nyhuis, is killed. A second jet from VF-112, embarked in USS *Philippine Sea* (CV-47), falls to AAA eight days later.

September China increases North Korean AAA strength in response to UN forces landing at Inchon.

November 9 First Task Force (TF) 77 strike on Yalu bridges. MiGs engage and claim two F9Fs, but only one (from VF-51) is lost in a landing accident when it has to take the barrier upon returning to *Valley Forge*.

November 10 First F9F-versus-MiG-15 combat. Lt Cdr William T. Amen of VF-111 shoots down Capt Mikhail F. Grachyov of 139th Guards Fighter Aviation Regiment for the first jet victory achieved by either side in the Korean War.

November 30 VMF-311 becomes the first Panther-equipped US Marine Corps squadron to arrive in Korea, flying from K-27 Yonpo.

December Soviet AAA and MiG-15 units are based in North Korea.

1951

January F9F-2Bs reach US Navy and US Marine Corps squadrons.

April 2 VF-191, embarked in USS *Princeton* (CV-37), undertakes the F9F-2B's first combat missions, including the first use of a US Navy jet as a fighter-bomber.

May Communist Spring Offensive begins.

Summer F9Fs from *Essex* fly B-29 escort missions.

VF-721 F9F-2s from *Boxer* overfly Wonsan on July 15, 1951 during the siege of the North Korean town. Wonsan airfield is just behind the Panther in the foreground. This aircraft is armed with both ATARs and HVARs. (US Navy)

September 28 First flight of the F9F-5P photo-reconnaissance aircraft.

October Soviet 82mm unguided rockets are fired, singly or in barrages, detonating at 10,000ft, but without damaging UN aircraft.

November F9F-5 deliveries begin.

1952

February KPA has four AAA divisions, 18 independent AAA regiments and 80 AAA battalions, with each of the latter also controlling 20 AA machine gun companies.

September F9F-5s enter the war with VF-781 and VF-783 (later re-designated VF-121 and VF-122, respectively), embarked in USS *Oriskany* (CVA-34).

1953

March 5 The death of Joseph Stalin leads to Soviet withdrawal from the conflict and Chinese reappraisal of their position in the light of possible US nuclear attacks on China.

July 27 An armistice is signed after more than 3.5 million military and civilian casualties on both sides.

1956

Summer F9F-2/3s leave operational fleet squadrons and are transferred to Reserve and training units.

1958

Spring Final two US Marine Corps units (VMF-213 and VMF-234) retire F9Fs.

Cpl Atlee Lemasters of the British Army's 71st Signal Service Battalion poses with a captured M1944 (KS-18), the KPA's primary heavy AAA weapon. He would have required six more team members to operate the 85mm gun, which could traverse through 360 degrees on its transport base and elevate to 82 degrees. (Imperial War Museum MH33272)

DESIGN AND DEVELOPMENT

F9F PANTHER

Grumman and its principal customer the US Navy, inspired by the USAAF's first jet fighter in the form of the Bell P-59 Airacomet, began to explore the possibilities of jet engines in 1943. As development of gas turbine engines in the USA had low wartime priority, American manufacturers were given access to imported British Halford H-1B (Goblin), Derwent, and Nene powerplants. Grumman was, by then, well established as principal supplier of US Navy fighters, with an extended series of piston-engined "cats" (F4F Wildcat, F6F Hellcat, F7F Tigercat and F8F Bearcat) having attained quantity production. Grumman hesitated over a jet propulsion program, however, fearing long, costly development and uncertain production numbers.

The company eventually initiated four studies for Design 75, a competitor for the US Navy's April 1945 requirement

The eighth production F9F-2 (BuNo 122567) was used by the Naval Air Test Center at NAS Patuxent River. (US Navy)

9

for a twin-jet, all-weather nightfighter. The G-75 version was a large, two-seat aircraft with straight wings, radar, and four 3,000lbs thrust Westinghouse 24C turbojets. The US Navy designated the aircraft XF9F-1, although it eventually chose the Douglas design which duly became the F3D Skyknight – a useful nightfighter in Korea. The US Navy incentivized Grumman jet projects by ordering two XF9F-1 prototypes as back-up for the Skyknight. It suggested that Grumman should, for the same contract value, substitute continued Tigercat production for another single-seat, jet-powered day fighter to meet its 1944 requirement.

The result was a variety of proposals titled Design 79. These included Study C, with a pair of Derwent engines, which resembled the British Gloster Meteor. Grumman used a turbojet in most of its "79" aircraft, with composite propeller-plus-Derwent-driven powerplants in two "tail-sitter" designs. Four manufacturers submitted proposals for the US Navy's second-generation jet fighter, including McDonnell, which received a contract for the XFD-2 that became the F2H Banshee. The latter would operate alongside the Panther in Korea. Contracts were also awarded to North American for the straight-winged XFJ-1 Fury, which evolved into another major Korean War jet fighter, the F-86 Sabre.

Grumman's Design 79D, a single-engined fighter with a 37ft-span straight wing and a gross weight of 12,400lbs, was feasible due to the unexpected availability of a superior engine to the Derwent. The RB.41 Nene was the most powerful jet engine of its time, inspired by two 4,000lbs thrust General Electric prototype designs which Sir Stanley Hooker of Rolls-Royce saw in the USA in 1944. It was simple, lightweight, and inexpensive, and it proved reliable in the British Attacker, Sea Hawk, and Vampire, although its centrifugal compressor design limited its potential power for fighters. Congress prevented direct imports of the British engine, but license-building agreements with Pratt & Whitney made Americanized versions available as the J42.

As Pratt & Whitney's historian recorded at the time, "The Nene offered more power and better reliability than any turbojet likely to appear soon on the American scene. Its rating of 5,000lbs thrust was attained with a total weight of 1,700lbs. It was the low weight/power ratio, plus its durability, that attracted the Navy to an Americanized version for a new jet fighter, the F9F. The Navy was also interested in stimulating competition among American engine manufacturers. So successful was the Nene in achieving this objective that it quickly became known as 'the Needle Engine'."

Pratt & Whitney negotiated with Rolls-Royce in 1947 to manufacture the engine as the J42-P-6, taking over a contract which had originally been given to the smaller Taylor Turbine Corporation. When it seemed that J42s might not be ready for the F9F-2's flight tests, Taylor handed over six British-built Nenes to Grumman. However, a J42-P-6 appeared in time for installation in the first production F9F-2

F9F-3 BuNo 122574 of VF-51 is carefully towed off a flightdeck elevator into CV-45's *Valley Forge*'s hangar bay during the early weeks of the Korean War. This aircraft was the third, and last, Panther lost by the unit during its first combat cruise, the jet being hit by AAA and its pilot forced to ditch on September 19, 1950. Budget constraints had shortened VF-51's transition from the FJ-1 Fury to the Panther, allowing time for just one weapons training deployment and no air-to-ground practice prior to the unit entering combat. (US Navy)

completed by Grumman on 24 November 1948.

The F9F-2 could trace its lineage back to August 1946, when the US Navy accepted Design 79D, which resembled Hawker's Nene-powered P.1040

Two VF-51 F9F-2s undertake a photo-escort mission for a VC-61 Det B F9F-2P in the fall of 1951. The pilot of the trailing jet is Ens Neil Armstrong, later to become the first man to set foot on the moon. Making his combat debut on August 29, 1951, Armstrong was shot down by AAA just five days later. The lead aircraft in this section is flown by Lt(jg) Ernie Russell. (US Navy)

Sea Hawk. Three 79D prototypes, redesignated XF9F-2s, were ordered. The US Navy's Head of Fighter Design, Cdr Alfred B. Metsger, wanted one to have swept wings, but Grumman agreed to present only basic swept wing design ideas. Instead, the third prototype tested an alternative engine, the heavier Allison J33-A-8, in case of restricted availability or technical problems with the Nene. Designated F9F-3, it was underpowered, with only 4,600lbs of thrust on take-off compared with the F9F-2's 5,750lbs.

During 1946, Grumman modified the tail surfaces, lengthened the tailpipe, and re-sited the cockpit further aft. Construction began in March 1947, and the first aircraft (BuNo 122475) began ground tests in October. Test pilot Corwin "Corky" Meyer flew it on November 21, taking the prototype over New York City to Idlewild Airport. On this and the return flight, Meyer was able to complete many of the basic handling tests. He found the Panther "very maneuverable. It gets to 10,000ft in a little over a minute." Its performance, including a 450mph dash on that first flight, was enhanced by having no armament or ejection seat and little naval equipment.

On August 16, 1948, the XF9F-3 (BuNo 122476) joined the test program. Grumman and US Navy tests revealed longitudinal instability throughout the speed range, particularly at lower speeds with light fuel loads. The aircraft "snaked," impeding gun-aiming and carrier landings. The short fuselage and small vertical tail were potential causes, remedied in the F9F-5. It was also found that fuel sloshed around in the fuselage tanks, affecting stability, so restraining baffles were fitted. Further lateral control problems arose with the hydraulically boosted ailerons, which were hard to operate in a manual reversion situation. Test pilots pushed the jet to Mach 0.85, but encountered major buffeting from Mach 0.83 onwards. Although the hydraulic boost system was a persistent maintenance problem throughout the Korean War, generally, pilots praised the Panther's handling qualities.

Chief US Navy test pilot Capt Frederick Trapnell also observed that the F9F-2/3 was unlikely to fulfil its estimated combat radius of 300 nautical miles. Recognizing the turbojet's increased fuel consumption compared with piston engines, several US manufacturers fitted wingtip tanks. They had no adverse effect on handling, acting as endplates, slightly increasing the wing area and adding 35 percent more fuel. The tanks, which extended mission times to more than 150 minutes, were removeable but not jettisonable. Emergency dump valves on their rear tips expelled the fuel in less than one minute.

Initial carrier suitability trials at the Naval Air Test Center involved the second prototype XF9F-2 (BuNo 122477), which was lost when the engine flamed out and would not re-start – a persistent problem that eventually required the igniter system

A captured KPA 85mm M1939 (52-K) KS-12. Later in the war, this weapon was supplemented by the similar M1944 KS-18 model, which featured a stronger recoil mechanism, a more powerful charge, and a higher muzzle velocity, enabling it to reach targets at 30,000ft. (USAF)

to be re-designed. The new jet's performance took a while to be assimilated on its first combat cruise aboard *Valley Forge*, as Lt Don Engen of VF-51 explained. "The ship's captain didn't understand why these jets had to land so fast. The [ship's] combat information center just couldn't cope with the speed. Their minds were boggled at the speed at which this blip would move across the horizon. Jets were still kind of an oddity."

There were also reservations about its high stalling speed, while increased fuel consumption (four times that of the propeller-driven F4Us the F9Fs shared the flightdeck with) meant pilots had to plan their flights and fuel needs carefully. Lt Engen devised an alternative to the complex fuel calculation tables in the pilot's handbook. "I remembered my language training, and when taking French I used a verb wheel. You could dial in a verb and get the English meaning. So I tinkered with a verb wheel and came up with an idea that I could design a fuel control computer that would be round, about four inches in diameter. By having my squadronmates record how much fuel they used at this altitude and that percent power, I could build a factual way of finding out how long you could fly an airplane. I ended up with a voluminous bunch of data."

Engen created a cardboard cruise-control calculator that became very useful to his squadron in Korea. Similar versions were widely used in the US Navy. Fuel efficiency was reduced by having to burn the heavier, more expensive aviation gasoline used by piston-engined types, rather than JP-1 kerosene. Gasoline also covered the turbine blades and tailpipes with toxic lead deposits that had to be scoured off by throwing walnut shells into the engine while it was idling. Fuel availability for VF-51's first combat cruise was a problem in itself, as Engen explained. "We would have to burn 115 and 145 aviation gasoline aboard ship because that's all they had. Then we'd suck it all up and they would be out of gas. So the 'props' were always mad at us because we'd take all the gas and we were forever having to refuel."

NORTH KOREAN AAA WEAPONS

North Korea's AAA equipment comprised obsolete, ex-Soviet designs dating from World War II or before, although many such weapons remained in use worldwide 30 years later. MiG-15 fighters arrived in-theater from November 1950, but guns were a more cost-effective way of providing North Korea with effective air defense. The introduction of radar guidance made the heavier weapons far more credible opposition to UN aircraft.

The SON-2 radar used to direct heavy AAA in North Korea had its origins in the 1935-vintage British GL ("gun-laying") Mk II radar. It employed similar principles to the Chain Home radar system – a crucial aid during the Battle of Britain – to

Designed during World War II, the Goryunov SG-43 7.62mm air-cooled machine gun was produced in China as the Type 53 and widely used in Korea. It was notable for its tilting breechblock mechanism. This example still served with Egyptian forces during Exercise *Bright Star* in 1985. (US Army/DoD)

determine the positions and headings of enemy aircraft. Separate transmitter and receiver units on gun carriages provided data on target elevation and bearing, accurate to within one degree. Each antenna registered a separate "blip" on a screen, and the operator's role was to manipulate the antennas to make both signals meet over the position of the stronger blip, so that they appeared to be of equal length.

Britain sent around 200 Mk IIs to the USSR in 1941, where they received the designation SON-2. Some of these were later passed to North Korea, where they were mainly allocated to AAA batteries along the west coast of the country and in the northwest. The SON-2 were often grouped together with searchlights, some of which were also radar-controlled.

American electronic countermeasure (ECM) equipment could jam SON-2, but it was a vital part of the SAC nuclear deterrent that could not initially be risked over North Korea in case its capabilities were revealed to Soviet advisors working with the KPA and NKPAF. When B-29 bomber losses mounted, they started to carry chaff bundles and jammers to block communist gun-laying radar. Communist gunners then had to resort to firing "blocking" box-barrages. When SAC relented and ECM was finally fielded by B-29s, the bombers' night-time losses were reduced by two-thirds.

BELOW LEFT
Communist forces relied on the SON-2 radar to guide its heavy AAA during the Korean War. The Soviet-built system was a copy of the British GL Mk II radar, around 200 of which were supplied to the USSR in 1941. (Public Domain)

BELOW RIGHT
The ZPU series, with between one and four 14.5mm barrels, was in service in the USSR from 1949 and soon appeared in Korea. The weapon was manned by a crew of four, and Chinese versions that served with the KPA and PVA were known as Type 58s. (Claudio_ne2000/Wiki Creative Commons)

TECHNICAL SPECIFICATIONS

F9F PANTHER

The US Marine Corps method (dubbed "Operation Hotfoot") of dealing with iced-up steel matting runways was to crank up and tow a grounded F9F with its tail section removed, letting the jet blast from its Pratt & Whitney J42-P-6 melt the ice. (US Marine Corps)

The first two F9F versions to enter fleet service, the F9F-2 (567 built) and F9F-3 (54 produced) differed only in the type of engine they used. The F9F-2's J42-P-4 (Nene) had nine compression chambers and produced 5,750lbs of thrust, increased to 5,950lbs for take-off by one-shot water/alcohol injection from a 22.5 gallons tank above the tailpipe. Test pilot Corky Meyer noted, "We'd get to about 100 knots, pour the water on and get a real kick in the butt. It only lasted about 30 seconds." Air conditioning was switched off when injection was in use to keep alcohol fumes out of the cockpit, but when it was re-engaged, a vision-obscuring cloud of condensation filled the cockpit.

The first F9F-2s had the J42-P-4. For operations from Essex-class aircraft carriers, which only carried piston-engined aviation fuel, the latter needed a three percent addition of lubricating oil to make it suitable for this engine. The later J42-P-6 was adjusted to burn aviation fuel without the oil additive. J42-P-8s with improved ignition systems appeared in many later F9F-2s. The F9F-3's less powerful Allison J33-A-8 was 200lbs heavier.

During the Panther's early combat use, pilots sometimes experienced alarming engine vibration caused by the turbine shedding a few blades. F9F-3s had no ordnance-carrying pylons – a major problem when VF-51 and VF-52 were tasked with contributing to the relief of UN troops confined in the Pusan area.

The Allison engine was also installed in the F9F-4, although J42s were substituted towards the end of the production run. Two large blow-in doors in the upper rear fuselage opened automatically to admit extra air for the engine on take-off and at low speeds. The engine could be accessed by removing the entire rear fuselage aft of the wing root. If the aircraft was hit in the aft fuselage, starting a fire, the tail section would soon blow off, rendering the Panther uncontrollable.

The F9F's straight wings had large hydraulically folding outer sections, reducing the span from 38ft to 23ft 5in. Two wingtip-mounted 120-gallon fuel tanks supplemented the 682 gallons contained in the F9F-2/3's two self-sealing fuselage tanks.

Lack of external ordnance capability was the biggest criticism of the early F9F-2 in combat, so from the modified F9F-2B onwards the wings each had four Mk 55 Mod 0 or superior Mod 1 bomb racks added, with an inboard Mk 51 Mod 0 bomb rack stressed for 1,000lb bombs. Outer pylons could each take 250lbs, including High Velocity Aerial Rockets (HVARs) on Aero 14A launchers, or Mks 57 and 64 bombs. The preferred weapon was the 250lb general purpose (GP) bomb, which did not affect the aircraft's stability when released. For flak suppression, a 250lb variable-time (VT) bomb wrapped with ten pounds of frangible steel straps and detonated by a radio-controlled fuse at a pre-set altitude, or delayed by up to six hours, was a devastating weapon. The F9F-2B designation later reverted, simply, to F9F-2.

The Panther's internal armament consisted of four Hispano-Suiza Mk 3 20mm cannon, each firing 190 rounds (ten per second) and charged by an Aero 13A hydraulic system. Two guns or all four could be selected. The US Navy preferred 20mm guns to the USAF's 0.50-cal machine guns, for although they were more likely to jam, the shells the weapons fired were more destructive in aerial combat.

Ammunition was fed from four boxes, two above the guns and two (outboard guns) below the pilot's seat. Maintainers found the latter location awkward to

Wingtip tanks were fueled directly with the wings folded by hanging a purpose-built ladder on each tank to reach its filler port. They had to be emptied before a carrier arrestment and were sometimes only partially filled to meet take-off weight requirements. Here, a VF-112 F9F-2 is being readied on the flightdeck of *Philippine Sea* in September 1950 during the unit's first combat cruise. (US Navy)

15

access, and repeatedly asked for all the boxes to be located in the nose. In the ten aircraft that typically equipped a fleet squadron, all four boxes were beneath the pilot's seat so as to allow for additional electronics to be installed in the nose. In 1953, *Oriskany's* ordnance report noted that "It requires approximately three times as long to re-arm the F9F-5 as to re-arm other types of aircraft [in the carrier air group] due to the design and placement of ammunition cans and feed chutes."

Cartridge cases and links were stored in a nose compartment to preserve the center of gravity. The entire nose cone slid forward on rails to access the armament and electronics (an AN/APG-30 ranging radar was placed above the guns in the F9F-5, working with a Mk 6 fire control system and an Aero 2C gunsight), although this could also "blow off" in early aircraft when the weapons were fired if gun-gas pressure built up in the nose. Venting louvers were duly added. In several cases where Panthers had to ditch, the nose section broke off, causing disintegration of the aircraft.

The guns' nose location required care while awaiting take-off. A US Marine Corps F9F got too close to the jet in front of it on the runway and hot engine efflux made some rounds "cook off," narrowly missing the Panther ahead. Korea's low winter temperatures also led to problems with the F9F-2's primary weapon, as *Philippine Sea's* December 1950 After Action Report noted. "The 20mm gun is one of the air group's greatest problems in the combat area during cold weather. One of the main problems is the freezing of condensed water on the gun parts and on the ammunition trays and cans."

In warmer conditions, it was found by *Valley Forge* F9F pilots to be "a devastating attack weapon," and far superior to the 0.50-cal machine gun for flak suppression. Proof of the weapons' success was recorded by an AN/N-6A gun camera installed in the starboard wing root. By 1953 refined maintenance routines and construction had improved reliability. Carrier Air Group (CVG) 12, embarked in *Oriskany*, reported in January 1953 that its F9F-5 guns each averaged 1,200 rounds before a stoppage.

The Panther's centrifugal jet engine required a wide fuselage that provided a comparatively spacious cockpit. The US Navy had only begun ejection seat tests in November 1946, and Grumman's seat used an early Martin-Baker design that had been modified by the Naval Air Engineering Center. Lt Don Engen and Lt(jg) Len Plog (who later shot down a Yak-9P to give the Panther its first aerial victory of the Korean War) were amongst the small group of Naval Aviators that tested the seat in mid-1949. The two pilots had also collected the first batch of F9F-3s, without ejection seats.

Ejection took several stages, making a safe escape at altitudes below 1,300ft unlikely – this fact did little to inspire confidence in the seat among pilots. In order to initiate ejection, the pilot first had to pull the

VMF-311's F9F-2 BuNo 125116 at K-3 Pohang armed with a World War II-vintage 11.74in. "Tiny Tim" unguided anti-shipping and "bunker buster" rocket, with a 150lb warhead, on its Mk 51 rack. It was ignited by a lanyard after dropping from the pylon and launched from beyond the range of AAA. The rocket upset a Panther's trim on catapult launch. Then Lt Wynn Foster recalled firing one while flying with VF-721 on board USS *Kearsarge* (CVA-33). "It sounded like a high-speed freight train going by. I was so fascinated watching it snake down towards the target that I almost flew into the side of a mountain." (US Marine Corps)

pre-ejection lever to jettison the cockpit canopy, release the safety pin, lower the seat, and activate its knee supports. Having drawn his feet back into stirrups on the seat's base, he pulled the overhead nylon rope handles to lower a protective curtain across his face, lock his harness, and fire the seat. Separation from the seat was manual after disconnecting the seat belt, radio leads and oxygen supply, and before pulling the parachute rip cord.

Standard flight kit included a separate G-suit, an inflatable Mae West, and a kneepad for mission notes. The parachute, stowed under a seat cushion together with survival gear for a bail-out over water, remained in the aircraft between missions.

The nose cone of an F9F-2B (with an extensive mission scoreboard) from VMF-311 has been slid forwards to access its guns while armorers fit 6.5in. ATARS beneath the wings. Spent ammunition cases dropped into the lower gun compartment section (which could also accommodate personal luggage on ferry flights) and were then collected in a canvas bag post-flight. (US Marine Corps)

Flying controls were operated by conventional cables and pulleys, with hydraulic boost for the ailerons. An electronic elevator trim device was introduced later, but it was difficult to set correctly for diving attacks in combat. Two sets of wing flaps were installed – an outboard set deflected by 40 degrees and an inboard set, beneath the fuselage, lowered by 45 degrees for take-off and 19 degrees for landing. Leading-edge flaps were provided to increase lift for take-off and landing. A manually raised "stinger" tailhook and a retractable safety skid extended below the rear fuselage to protect the tailpipe during arrestment.

The main landing gear units retracted inwards into the center fuselage, while the nose gear, strengthened after early carrier experience of fractures, folded backwards.

F9F-2/3s impressed pilots with their typical strong Grumman structure, although their Mach limitations had to be observed carefully. The maximum was Mach 0.83 in a dive, accompanied by considerable buffeting and a tendency to pitch up suddenly. Beyond Mach 0.79 instability, sudden trim changes, and buffeting occurred.

For the F9F-5, Pratt & Whitney asked Rolls-Royce to develop a more powerful engine. Although the company was already heavily committed to its new Avon axial flow powerplant, Rolls-Royce's developed Tay design was passed on to Pratt & Whitney as the J48 for further evolution and license production. With a much-improved thrust of 6,250lbs in its P-6A version, the engine was 30 percent larger than the Nene. Its fuel pump system adjusted to altitude and engine speed, but early versions of its turbojet controller could freeze, allowing excess fuel into the engine so that it began un-commanded acceleration. Throttling back to idle and reverting to manual fuel control was the only way to avert an explosion. The J48's extra power raised the Panther's top combat speed to 579mph at 5,000ft, and it became the first US Navy fighter capable of exceeding 600mph in level flight. Higher fuel consumption slightly reduced range.

1. Canopy control (normal, hydraulic)
2. Take-off check-off list
3. Tailpipe temperature indicator
4. Canopy control (emergency air)
5. Fuel and oil pressure indicator
6. Low fuel boost pressure warning light
7. Armament switch panel
8. Tachometer
9. Mk 8 Mod 0 gunsight
10. Maximum allowable airspeed indicator
11. Gyro-horizon
12. Rate-of-climb indicator
13. Standby compass
14. Fuel quantity indicator
15. Low-level fuel warning light
16. Clock
17. Landing check-off list
18. Arresting hook control
19. Arresting hook indicator light
20. Cabin altimeter
21. Sliding nose unlocked warning sign
22. Accelerometer
23. Arresting hook raising switch button
24. Fire warning light
25. Compass correction card
26. Radio compass
27. Turn-and-bank indicator
28. Compass correction card
29. G-2 compass
30. Control column (trigger button on grip)
31. Altimeter
32. Radio altimeter indicator
33. Airspeed correction card
34. Landing gear down lock solenoid emergency manual release
35. Landing gear unlocked warning light
36. Landing gear control lever
37. Landing gear emergency "T" handle
38. G-suit valve control
39. Radio altimeter selector switch
40. Oxygen regulator
41. Air start switch on/off button
42. Wingtip tank fuel dump switch
43. Wingtip tank fuel flow warning lights
44. Right wingtip tank flow switch
45. Left wingtip tank flow switch
46. J33-A-8 engine control switch panel

The F9F-4 was developed at the same time as the "Dash Five," with the jet being powered by the Allison J33-A-16. This engine quickly proved to be both unreliable and underpowered, so it was replaced by the J48-P-6.

The F9F-4/5's fuselage was lengthened by 19in. ahead of the wing root to allow for 80 gallons of extra fuel for the more demanding J48. Its air intakes were redesigned with a small aerodynamic fence just outboard from the intake to reduce stalling speed. Maximum carrier take-off weight from improved Mk 8 catapults increased to 20,600lbs, including 2,500lbs of ordnance compared with 16,450lbs for the F9F-2. In 1953, *Oriskany* was able to launch its F9F-5s with 2,750lbs of ordnance. The aircraft's extra weight made operations from the catapults fitted to

VMF-115 F9F-2Bs, each armed with six 250lb bombs, taxi out for a March 1953 mission from Pohang. This war load was favored for flak suppression. The metal Marston Matting used at USAF airfields was very hard on tires, with *Princeton*'s Panthers getting through 159 main landing gear tires in 43 days due to frequent weather diversions to K-18 Kangnung. (US Marine Corps)

47. J33-A-8 engine emergency fuel system check switch
48. J33-A-8 engine starting switch guard
49. Wing flaps control
50. Automatic Fire Control System switch
51. Aileron booster emergency on-off control
52. Fuel master switch
53. Water injection quantity indicator
54. Wheel and flap position indicator
55. 55. Water injection pressure indicator
56. Water injection switch
57. Wing leading edge position indicator
58. Dive brake control
59. Throttle (with microphone button)
60. Aileron trim tab control
61. Rudder trim tab control
62. Elevator tab control wheel
63. Emergency brake "T" handle
64. Hydraulic system pressure gauge
65. Map case
66. C-115/ARC-1 control switches
67. C-268/ARC-19
68. C-115/ARC-1
69. C-268/ARC-19 control switches
70. Circuit breaker re-set button panel
71. Electrical test pin jacks
72. Seat height control
73. Interior lights switch panel
74. Exterior lights switch panel
75. G-2 compass switch
76. Cabin pressurizing control panel
77. Generator on/off switch
78. Battery switch
79. Generator warning light
80. Pitot heater switch
81. Volt/ammeter
82. C-119/APX-1 or -1A control panel
83. C-149/ARN-6 control panel
84. Radio master switch panel
85. Hydraulic system shut-off control (combat – normal)
86. Spare lamp container
87. Wing lock control
88. Wing folding control
89. Hydraulic auxiliary pump pressure gauge
90. Hydraulic emergency auxiliary pump switch

Essex-class carriers more difficult. When VF-111's F9F-5s embarked in *Boxer* in March 1953, they were soon transferred to USS *Lake Champlain* (CVA-39), the only Essex-class carrier to see combat in the Korea War with Class 27 updates, which included more powerful catapults.

The extended fuselage necessitated a vertical tail that was 12in. taller and increased in area to preserve stability. Also, the wing aerofoil section was reduced from 12 percent to 10 percent thickness to lower drag at high speeds, while the speed brakes were revised to operate together with a section of the flaps. The wings were strengthened for extra ordnance-carrying capacity of 500lbs per outer Aero 14A rack. The inboard pylons could take 150-gallon external fuel tanks, sometimes fitted to the F9F-5P. External ordnance was increased to around 4,000lbs, rather than 2,800lbs for the F9F-2/3. A total of 1,382 F9F-4/5s were manufactured, making it the most numerous Panther variant.

Grumman also provided the US Navy with its first jet photo-reconnaissance aircraft, converting 36 F9F-2s into F9F-2Ps – most went to Composite Squadron (VC) 61. Their two camera bays replaced the guns and fire control system. The forward bay contained a fixed vertical camera (usually a Fairchild K-17) and the rear bay housed a rotary-mounted, oblique-angled K-17 or wider-angle K-18 camera with 6in. or 12in. lenses. A trimetrogon arrangement of three 6in. cameras could operate through three windows below and to each side of the nose. Access to the cameras was via the sliding nose section and a large panel above the nose. Ballast compensated for the weight of the discarded armament, while the weapons controls were replaced by an A-10VF photo-viewfinder and controls for the photo-recorder and flasher unit.

The converted F9F-2Ps were followed by 36 purpose-built F9F-5Ps. Their noses were extended by 12in. to allow more room for cameras, including photographic mapping capability. A General Electric G-3 autopilot was also installed.

F9F-2 Panther Specification	
Dimensions	
Length	37ft 5in.
Wingspan	38ft 0in.
Height	11ft 4in.
Wing area	250ft²
Weights	
Empty	9,909lbs
Max take-off	19,494lbs
Performance	
Max speed	575mph at sea level
Initial rate of climb	5,140ft per minute
Service ceiling	44,600ft
Range	1,354 miles (with external fuel)
Powerplant	one Pratt & Whitney J42-P-6 (5,750lbs thrust) turbojet engine

F9F-5 PANTHER

38ft 10.5in.

NAVY
VF153
F9F-5
NAVY
126230

313 JR

H

12ft 4in.

313 JR H

NAVY

38ft 0in.

COMMUNIST AAA WEAPONS

The heavier guns, including the big KS-19 100mm weapon, defended high-priority fixed targets in North Korea, with the M1938 and M1939 (52-K) KS-12 as the most numerous AAA pieces. The Soviet M1938 76.2mm gun was an improved version of the M1931 that was still in service in 1941. Inspired by pre-war British Vickers designs, a few were produced for use in World War II, although they were soon replaced by the 85mm KS-12. Many captured M1938s were used by the Germans following the invasion of the Soviet Union in June 1941, and a few found their way to North Korea post-war. Indeed, 20 were positioned mainly around the North Korean capital, Pyongyang, although only three were radar-controlled.

For fire control of the M1938 and other weapons, the PUAZO-3 optical director was used. By operating one hand-wheel for elevation and a second to control azimuth position, the target was placed within crosshairs in the telescopic sight – this could also be achieved using a DYA four-meter base range finder. As long as a target was kept within the sight, information on its location could be sent electrically to direct a gun equipped with automatic electrical drive. The M1938 and 85mm KS-12 used a manual system with two pointers on the gun, one showing the values on elevation and azimuth supplied by the PUAZO-3 and the second showing information on where the gun was pointing. Gunners then had to align the two pointers to match the PUAZO's values, although range was often judged by the gun commander based on his experience.

The Soviet PUAZO-6 optical AAA fire director was a basic mechanical computer with a reflex visual sight. Like other components in the air defense armory, it could be transported by road. (Bukvoed/Public Domain)

M1939 (52-K) KS-12 85mm heavy AAA guns were normally located in batteries of four or eight, often with a gun-laying radar unit providing target guidance. The KPA and PVA also occasionally used these weapons as field artillery against advancing US troops. (Public Domain)

The PUAZO unit, weighing more than 5,700lbs on its transport device, could produce guide values for targets at altitudes of more than 25,000ft. However, its optical rangefinder limited its use to daylight except when searchlights were available, and it was useless in poor weather or against maneuvering targets. Units supplied to the NKA could be used with SON-2 or SON-3 radars in darkness, but the PUAZO was generally ineffective against fast jets like the Panther. It required an 11-man team of operators, and in North Korea the PUAZO was generally used in conjunction with KS-12 guns.

The M1938 was scaled up as the M1939 (52-K) KS-12 85mm towed gun, and it quickly became the NKA's principal heavy AAA weapon. A crew of seven operated the gun, which fired 20.5lb cartridges – each shell contained 1.4lbs of high explosive, detonated by a proximity fuse. A single hit would normally cripple an aircraft. The gun was known for its accuracy, and it had an effective range of 20,000ft. The KS-12 could, in fact, fire shells up to an altitude of 34,000ft. Like all Soviet guns, it originally had a dual role as an anti-tank weapon, and the KS-12 – in modified form – also served as the main armament of the T-34-85 medium tank and SU-85 tank destroyer.

The Soviet-designed 57mm S-60 towed gun was produced in China as the Type 59 and widely used during the war. Weighing five tons, it fired manually-fed, four-round clips of ammunition at around 70 rounds per minute. The gun's mount allowed it to turn through 360 degrees and elevate to 90 degrees. The principal automatic AAA weapon was the 37mm M1939 (61-K), derived from the Bofors 25mm Model 1933. Its ammunition was similar in size to the 37mm (1.45in.) ordnance fired by the Colt-Browning M1 AAA weapon that was replaced in US Army service by the Bofors gun from 1943.

The M1939, which fired a five-round ammunition clip, needed a commander and a crew of seven to load it and operate the fire-control system, using an inbuilt computing sight. Target range (from 660 to 13,200ft), target speed (up to 300mph), and course were fed into the computer, which calculated appropriate deflection angles for azimuth and elevation, passing this data to the gunsight. The M1939's effective range was around 4,500ft, and its speed of operation (up to 180 rounds per minute, but more usually 80 rounds per minute), high muzzle velocity, and weight of fire compared with a medium or heavy artillery weapon made it lethal against fast-moving targets, particularly at lower altitudes.

The 37mm M1939 (61-K) AAA weapon was a pre-World War II Soviet design that was also manufactured in China as the Type 55 and supplied to North Korea to supplement its M1938s. (Public Domain)

The gun's simple construction ("agricultural" in the opinion of one pilot, particularly in reference to its tractor-like seats) and rugged four-wheel transport carriage made it highly mobile and easy to operate with minimal training. It could be a devastating weapon. An F7F Tigercat returned to K-14 Kimpo from a close air support (CAS) mission with a 4ft x 2ft foot hole in its wing from a single hit. Pilots recognized the M1939's presence by the white puffs of exploding ammunition.

The KPA also fielded a number of 25mm M1941 guns. Copied from a Bofors design, this single- or dual-mounted weapon could fire shells at 240 rounds per minute up to an altitude of 4,000ft. The ubiquitous 12.7mm DShKM 1938 machine gun,

31ft

7ft 8in.

KS-19

The KS-19 100mm gun was the largest AAA weapon fielded by communist forces in Korea. Located around a number of high-value strategic targets, the KS-19 normally operated in conjunction with the SON-9 "Fire Can" guidance system. A well-coordinated 15-man crew was capable of firing 15 single rounds per minute from the weapon. Timed-fuse shells could reach beyond 41,000ft, putting USAF B-29 Superfortress heavy bombers at risk. Weighing 21,054lbs, the KS-19 was less frequently transported than smaller-caliber guns.

5ft 3in.

lethal at ranges up to 2,400ft, was used both in the AA role and as a general-purpose gun. Although the weapon could be fitted with a ring sight for anti-aircraft use, gunners operating DShKM 1938s tended to use tracer rounds as an aiming method at ranges up to 1,800ft.

Various small-arms and light machine guns were also in use, together with some 40mm weapons. The latter were probably captured Bofors guns acquired via Hungary, while a number of Type 5 equivalents built by Japan during World War II were also seized in September 1945. The KPA also used a handful of 40mm 40/40 V34 guns acquired by the USSR from Finland and passed on to North Korea. These veteran weapons were a distant descendant of the British 1920s-era Vickers 2-pounder, developed in Sweden and capable of firing 2lb shells up to 12,500ft at a rate of 120 rounds per minute.

The radar systems used by the North Koreans to guide many of these weapons came from a variety of sources. Although the majority of them was supplied by the USSR, AAA batteries also used Japanese Tachi 18 equipment, British AA Nos. 2 and 4 early warning and searchlight control sets, and SCR-270s from the USA (or the Soviet copy, known as "Whiff"). The KPA also fielded Soviet RUS-2 and P2M

KPA rifles and machine gun ammunition captured from a sampan off the Korean coast in 1951. Small-arms fired in concentrated blocks by infantrymen fighting on the frontline could bring a low-flying fighter-bomber down, although piston-engined types were more vulnerable to this than jets like the F9F. (US Navy)

Pegmantit early warning sets, together with "Dumbo" and "Token" early warning and ground-control interception radars.

Communist radar used during the Korean War was generally mobile, which meant it could be moved to within four miles of the frontline. US Navy crews undertaking "ferret" ECM flights reckoned that the radar operators were well trained. Standard practice, as would subsequently be the case during the Vietnam War, was to make a few sweeps with the scanner and then switch the radar off before its position could be determined by ECM aircraft like the US Navy's AD-2/4Q Skyraiders. As late as June 16, 1952, TF 77 squadrons finally began to use chaff to confuse the radar operators.

Invented in 1884 as the first production automatic weapon, the Maxim machine gun was still in service on the Soviet border a century later. It was also used by both sides in Korea, with the communists routinely employing it as an ad hoc AA weapon. This example was captured by British troops in September 1951. The Maxim's reliability was partly due to its water cooling. One example was tested in 1963 by firing more than five million rounds during a week of intensive tests. It subsequently required no repairs or maintenance. (Public Domain)

THE STRATEGIC SITUATION

When 128,000 troops of the KPA crossed the 38th parallel into South Korea on June 25, 1950 on the pretext that South Korea had already instigated an invasion of North Korea, the USAF's Far East Air Force (FEAF) had no direct responsibility for defending South Korea. It was committed instead to protecting Japan, the Marianas, and the Philippines with three fighter bomber wings, an interceptor wing and two light bomber squadrons, none of which were in South Korea. This all changed on June 26 when a UN Security Council resolution obliged the FEAF to support Republic of Korea (RoK) forces in their failing attempt to defend South Korea.

Rather than ignore the threat, or resort to nuclear weapons, the US government, already tired of war, had no option other than to engage the USSR's 'surrogate armies' in conventional warfare, even though Korea, in Secretary of State Dean Acheson's words, was "the worst possible place to fight a war."

Combat missions began on June 28, with attacks on railyards near Seoul and communist troops and armor on the surrounding roads. Good results persuaded President Harry S. Truman to authorize air strikes on targets in North Korea (at a safe distance from Manchuria and the USSR) and establish a naval blockade of northern ports. On June 29 FEAF leaders agreed that the best way to counteract the Soviet-backed North Korean advance was to use CVG-5, embarked in *Valley Forge*, to hit targets around Pyongyang. Airfields, railways in and around Kumchon, Sariwon, and Sinanju, and bridges over the Yalu River were also prioritized.

Valley Forge, an updated Essex-class vessel some 873ft in length, was the only US Navy carrier in Vice-Adm Arthur D. Struble's Seventh Fleet when the war began.

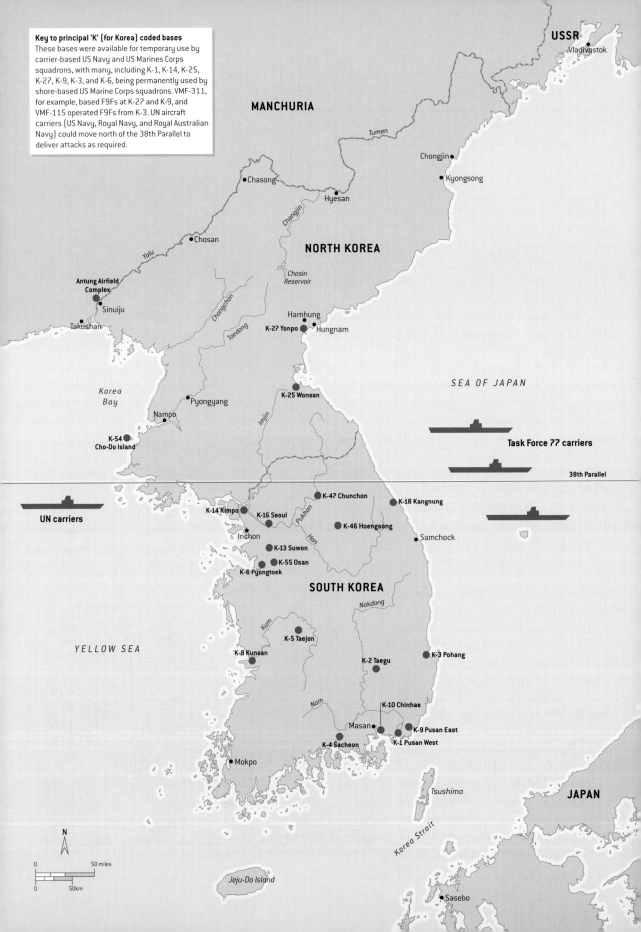

Key to principal 'K' (for Korea) coded bases
These bases were available for temporary use by carrier-based US Navy and US Marines Corps squadrons, with many, including K-1, K-14, K-25, K-27, K-9, K-3, and K-6, being permanently used by shore-based US Marine Corps squadrons. VMF-311, for example, based F9Fs at K-27 and K-9, and VMF-115 operated F9Fs from K-3. UN aircraft carriers (US Navy, Royal Navy, and Royal Australian Navy) could move north of the 38th Parallel to deliver attacks as required.

USSR

Vladivostok

MANCHURIA

Tumen

Chongjin

Chasong

Kyongsong

Hyesan

Chongjin

NORTH KOREA

Chosin
Reservoir

Chosan

Yalu

Antung Airfield
Complex

Changchon

Sinuiju

Taedong

Hamhung

Takushan

K-27 Yonpo

Hungnam

Korea
Bay

Pyongyang

K-25 Wonsan

SEA OF JAPAN

Nampo

Imjin

Task Force 77 carriers

K-54
Cho-Do Island

38th Parallel

K-47 Chunchon

K-18 Kangnung

UN carriers

K-14 Kimpo

K-16 Seoul

Pukhon

K-46 Hoengsong

Inchon

Han

Samchock

K-13 Suwon

K-55 Osan

K-6 Pyongtoek

SOUTH KOREA

Nakdong

YELLOW SEA

Kum

K-5 Taejon

K-8 Kunsan

K-2 Taegu

K-3 Pohang

Nam

K-10 Chinhae

Masan

K-9 Pusan East

K-4 Sacheon

K-1 Pusan West

Mokpo

Tsushima

JAPAN

N

Korea Strait

0   50 miles

0   50km

Jeju-Do Island

Sasebo

It duly headed for the North Korean coast from the South China Sea, via a hasty replenishment at Subic Bay, in the Philippines, in order to reinforce the FEAF. CVG-5 included the F9F-3s of VF-51 and VF-53 within the aircraft embarked in the carrier, the two fighter squadrons effectively working as one aboard ship, interchanging jets and sharing a maintenance officer and ready room.

A number of the US Navy's carriers and their aircraft were in long-term storage following service in World War II, and they had to be rapidly returned to operational status. *Valley Forge* was joined by the Royal Navy's light carrier HMS *Triumph*, with two squadrons flying Seafire FR 47s and Firefly FR 1s. Both Fleet Air Arm units began attacks on the NKPAF's Kaishu airfield on July 3, with combat air patrol (CAP) duties fulfilled by aircraft from CVG-5 as the carriers cruised within 100 miles of People's Liberation Army Air Force airfields. In follow-up afternoon attacks on Heiju airfield, near Pyongyang, by *Valley Forge*'s carrier air group, eight Panthers took part and scored the first aerial kills credited to US Navy jets. They also destroyed nine aircraft on the ground after encountering very little AAA opposition.

UN air superiority was quickly established over the small NKPAF, which had expected only token opposition from the even smaller Republic of Korea Air Force (RoKAF). Having secured control of the skies, US Navy aircraft carriers could now operate very closely to both west and east coasts of Korea.

Although railway and bridge attacks took place during July, the available air power was mainly needed for direct attacks on enemy troop concentrations. From July 28 coordinated attacks on communications began, based on the assertion by the FEAF's commanding general, Lt Gen George E. Stratemeyer, that the destruction of key bridges behind enemy lines was to be the primary objective of his force. B-29 bombers were the main weapons employed in the achievement of this aim, hitting marshaling yards, choke points and bridges at crucial locations on the network. Some bridges took a whole month of daily attacks (with bombs totaling 643 tons in the case of a steel bridge in Seoul) before they were deemed to have been destroyed.

Naval aircraft, with USAF fighter-bombers operating from Japanese bases, were allocated CAS and local interdiction missions in view of their limited range and smaller weapons loads. Often, they would be given a main target such as a bridge, and then expend any remaining ordnance on rolling stock or maintenance facilities. In late July the carrier *Boxer* arrived with 145 USAF F-51D Mustangs as deck cargo, these veteran aircraft formerly in service with Air National Guard and Air Force Reserve units being rushed into action from temporary airstrips at K-2 Taegu and K-3 Pohang.

The Mustangs supplemented the US Navy's air-to-ground effort to save beleaguered UN forces when they retreated into the "Pusan Perimeter" – a small area in the southeast of Korea – in early August.

A bridge at Sinuiju comes under attack in November 1950 by aircraft from CVG-3, embarked in *Leyte*. Amongst the aircraft involved in the mission were F9F-2s from VF-31 – the sole Panther-equipped unit within the carrier air group. Three spans of the road bridge have been dropped, while the many craters on the North Korean side of the Yalu attest to numerous attacks. AAA batteries on the Chinese side of the river could fire at US Navy aircraft with total impunity. (US Navy)

Carriers had by then become essential "floating airfields" for counter strikes in the absence of adequate land bases on the Korean mainland. Politically, such operations benefited the US Navy, which had been involved in a losing battle with the USAF for funding since the late 1940s.

By mid-1951 TF 77 usually had three carriers on station, with two in action and a third replenishing at sea. A fourth was kept in port in Japan at 12 hours' notice for emergencies. Essex-class carriers embarked either 18 F9F-2 or F2H-2 fighters, which supported a strike force of 32 Corsairs, split between two squadrons, and 16 Skyraiders in a solitary unit, with other small, specialist nightfighting, reconnaissance, ECM, and early warning detachments also embarked. By 1953 one of the Corsair squadrons had been replaced by a second Panther or Banshee unit so that 40 percent of the carrier air group consisted of jets.

INTERDICTION

FEAF tactics in Korea prioritized interdicting enemy transport and communications – a policy that echoed World War II's Operation *Strangle* during the 1944 Italian campaign, when Allied forces attempted to penetrate the Germans' "Gustav Line" defensive barrier across central Italy. This operational title was resurrected in May 1951 for the Fifth Air Force's interdiction assault on North Korea's transport network, which had the same aim of degrading supply routes and troop movements.

In a land of mountains and rivers, the establishment of rail and road routes in Korea had required immense civil engineering works. The central mountain ranges effectively split the rail networks into separate east and west coast systems, with the latter running along the Yellow Sea coastline, with river deltas which cause frequent flooding. In 1950 the whole of Korea had only 20 miles of paved road, near Seoul. North Korea lacked vehicles and suffered acute fuel shortages. This in turn meant that it relied more on rail transport, using an extensive network of 3,800 miles of track laid during the Japanese occupation, which lasted from 1904 through to 1945.

Strafing with 20mm guns could be devastating for transport targets. This ammunition-carrying train was destroyed on September 21, 1950. North Korean railwaymen soon became adept at hiding trains in tunnels during daylight hours. (NARA)

The FEAF divided North Korea into eight zones. The US Navy took two in central Korea, while three in the east were assigned to the US Marines Corps. Major railheads and bridges north of these zones were excluded from attack, although road transport was targeted as most movement in these areas was by truck. Roads and railway lines were patrolled by fighter-bombers, who damaged them with 500lb bombs and then dropped delayed-action M83 anti-personnel bombs to deter their repair.

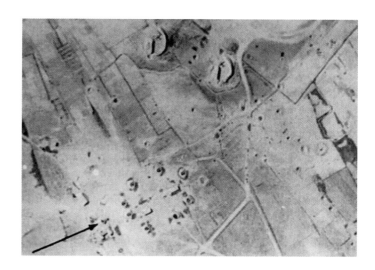

The interdiction campaign intensified after the UN's amphibious invasion of Inchon, codenamed Operation *Chromite*, in September 1950. Its aims were to secure Seoul and K-14 Kimpo airfield, to cut the enemy's communication lines and reinforcement routes, and isolate and destroy KPA forces south of a line from Inchon to Seoul. The air assets assigned to *Chromite* included four F9F squadrons among 19 strike and fighter units embarked in five US Navy carriers and HMS *Triumph*.

An eight-gun battery of heavy AAA in a circular site (marked with a black arrow on the original print) close to the end of the runway at Sinuiju airfield in North Korea – note the aircraft in two revetments at the top of the image. For high-risk targets like the Sui-ho hydroelectric dam, bridges at Sinanju, Antung and Siniuju airfields, and Pyongyang, batteries of 20–30 mobile searchlight units were also deployed, illuminating targets at 30,000ft for night-flying MiG-15s and AAA. (USAF)

By November 1950 communist forces had retreated to the Chongchon River, 60 miles from the Manchurian border. UN troops who had been enclosed at Pusan then advanced northwards to join the Inchon invasion force. During the effort to break out of the "Pusan Perimeter," US Navy and US Marine CAS was crucial. *Valley Forge* and *Philippine Sea* were positioned off the Korean coast to strike at North Korean advances. F4U Corsairs, embarked in the escort carriers USS *Badoeng Strait* (CVE-116) and USS *Sicily* (CVE-118), flew the majority of the CAS missions, totaling 6,575 flight hours against just 727 for the F9F squadrons.

The success of *Chromite* allowed the temporary cancellation of attacks on North Korean targets while the interdiction effort focused on the retreating KPA forces. Further destruction of communications was halted as it impeded UN troops as they moved northwards in pursuit of enemy forces. Repairs to South Korean rail networks began in October 1950. As the remaining communist troops reached the Yalu River on October 26, it became apparent that they included Chinese People's Volunteer Army (PVA) soldiers within their ranks. The extent of Chinese participation became clearer in December, when a UN Security Council report revealed that seven PVA armies numbering up to 250,000 men were with KPA forces south of the Yalu and pushing UN troops back once again.

China's entry into South Korea was eased because Commander-in-Chief of the UN Command, Gen Douglas MacArthur, had been refused permission to bomb the five rail bridges across the Yalu River. Approval was finally given on November 6, and USAF bombers, assisted by TF 77 aircraft, attacked the South Korean ends of the bridges and their AAA defenses. Sixty percent of the town of Sinuiju was also destroyed, with terrible loss of life.

The previous month, a fourth carrier had been added to TF 77 when USS *Leyte* (CV-32) arrived from the Mediterranean with Panther squadron VF-31 embarked as

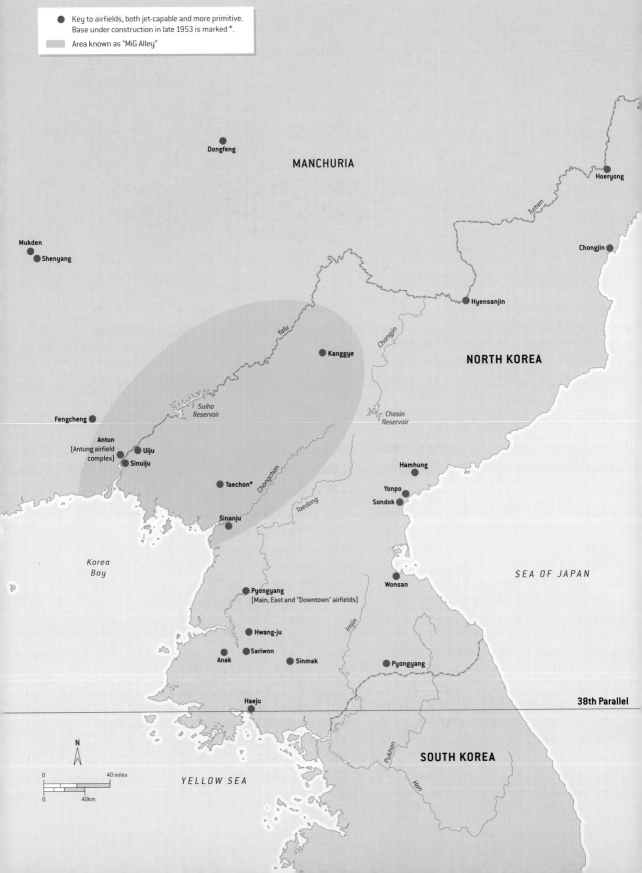

● Key to airfields, both jet-capable and more primitive.
Base under construction in late 1953 is marked *.

▨ Area known as "MiG Alley"

Dongfeng

MANCHURIA

Hoeryong

Tumen

Mukden
● Shenyang

Chongjin

Hyensanjin

Chongjin

Yalu

● Kanggye

NORTH KOREA

Fengcheng ●

Suiho
Reservoir

Chosin
Reservoir

Antun
(Antung airfield
complex)
● Uiju
● Sinuiju

Chongchon

● Hamhung
● Yonpo
Sondok ●

● Taechon*

Toedong

● Sinanju

Korea
Bay

SEA OF JAPAN

● Wonsan

● Pyongyang
(Main, East and "Downtown" airfields)

● Hwang-ju

Imjin

● Sariwon
Anak ●   ● Sinmak

● Pyongyang

● Haeju

38th Parallel

N

0   40 miles

0   40km

YELLOW SEA

Pukhan

SOUTH KOREA

Han

part of CVG-3, which contributed to strikes in the Wonsan area. F9F units provided up to 16 jets for target CAP (TARCAP) over bridges that were being attacked, while flak suppression was allotted to 16 Corsairs.

As the PVA, led by Gen Peng Dehuai, pushed relentlessly southwards without air cover or significant AAA protection, UN air power became the crucial element in blunting their advance, despite the loss of useable airfields in Korea that forced USAF aircraft to revert to operating from Japan again. Although bereft of heavy-caliber weapons, Chinese troops had adequate automatic AAA and small arms to have downed six F4U-4s undertaking CAS by December 1. Nevertheless, a lack of heavy AAA made the USAF's withdrawal of aircraft and personnel from K-14 Kimpo possible without significant losses in men and materiel.

KPA troops receive instruction in the use of machine guns in 1953. KPA rifle regiment soldiers were told to use half their weapons against air attacks in support of both dedicated AA units and their solitary 12.7mm machine gun section per battalion. (Sovfoto/ Universal Images Group via Getty Images)

From December 15, with the Yalu bridges still useable by Chinese troops despite intensive bombing, TF 77 was allocated three interdiction zones in the east of the country from Wonsan to the Siberian border. The priority targets were railway bridges and track.

By January 25, 1951, Chinese troops had over-extended their supply lines and they were forced to regroup, allowing a major UN offensive to be launched aimed at pushing them northwards. Around half of subsequent enemy casualties were caused by air attacks. The lack of UN bases on the Korean mainland allowed Soviet MiG-15 interceptors operating in "MiG Alley" (the area north of the Changchon River at Pyongyang across to the Yalu River) to intervene, blunting the efforts of the FEAF. Nevertheless, in February, B-29s were called in to destroy three railway bridges despite there being a reduced number of fighters available to escort them on daylight bombing operations. This only improved when K-13 Suwon and K-2 Taegu airfields were recaptured and quickly occupied by the 4th Fighter Wing's F-86A Sabres.

TF 77 aircraft, which had been diverted to CAS missions in an effort to stop the advancing PVA, were allowed to resume long-range interdiction in their eastern zones from February 6. They returned to targeting rail routes, which the communists had been forced to use at night due to persistent air attacks. Vice-Adm C. Turner Joy, Commander Naval Forces, Far East, argued that the railways in those areas were "of continuing value as a major route over which supplies, equipment, and troops are being transported to the immediate battle area". He emphasized the speed with which the enemy repaired these lines, and asserted that constant re-attacks were vital. "Naval air and naval gunfire are good weapons to accomplish this job," stated Vice-Adm Joy. Cuts in railway lines by bombing were generally being repaired within eight hours by a massive labor force.

Revised tactics were required in April 1951 when China threatened to invade Formosa, compelling TF 77 carriers to interrupt their interdiction activities and sail to the China Sea. By the time they returned to the Korean theater, the communist

Spring Offensive had begun and air power assets were again diverted to CAS. Nevertheless, US Navy aircraft mounted strikes against 31 bridges between Wonsan and Chongjin.

With FEAF aircraft concentrating on supporting UN troops attempting to halt the offensive, KPA and PVA engineers took the opportunity to repair communications routes. Following their endeavors, most railway rail lines were completely serviceable within a few months. Routes in the US Navy's eastern sectors were soon handling numerous freight cars, and heavy troop concentrations were found on lines from Hoeryong to Chongjin and Hamhung to Wonsan.

A second enemy counter-offensive began on 22 April, with 337,000 troops attempting to re-capture Seoul and cut off US forces in the west of South Korea. The attack was frustrated within a week, and UN forces were able to penetrate enemy rear areas with tanks, destroying supplies and causing heavy casualties. Further, less determined counteroffensives were also driven back, and by June 10 UN forces had established positions along the whole 38th parallel – a situation that was sustained until the end of hostilities. CAS by US Navy and USAF units had played a vital role in stopping these counter-offensives in May 1951, resulting in very heavy enemy casualties.

With the frontline now stabilized, the interdiction effort ramped up once again. It would continue at a high tempo until the end of hostilities in an effort to prevent substantial repairs being undertaken on bomb-damaged railway lines and route infrastructure. More than 14,200 wagons and 893 locomotives were destroyed or seriously damaged and only one bridge, between the Soviet-manned airfields at Antung (now Dandong) and Sinuiju, remained open.

Despite the damage inflicted on North Korea railways, Operation *Strangle* was considered unsuccessful because mission planners had targeted road transport links and ignored much of the rail network passing through Manchuria. Furthermore, there were still a number of intact bridges spanning the Yalu River. Random attacks on such

F9F-2 BuNo 123469 'PAPASAN' of VF-71 overflies the TF 77 carriers *Bon Homme Richard, Essex,* and *Princeton*, with their accompanying ships, off the Korean coast in August 1952. VF-71 was assigned to CVG-7 embarked in *Bon Homme Richard*. (National Archives)

targets without overall control of the relevant forces involved and the incompatibility of USAF and US Navy radio equipment fitted in combat aircraft in-theater were problems that also needed to be resolved.

A second interdiction phase from August 1951 re-emphasized rail attacks by fighter-bombers to prevent railways, including those in Manchuria, from being maintained in operable condition. This policy also resulted in a massive increase in the AAA defenses deployed to defend targets that had been repeatedly hit during *Strangle*. Additional sorties were duly allocated for the suppression of heavy-caliber AAA sites, but losses mounted. From October 1, 1951 through to January 1, 1952, ground fire accounted for 111 UN aircraft (including three Panthers). AAA also reduced the accuracy of bombing, forcing pilots to employ dive attacks from higher altitudes. MiG opposition became more determined and men and materiel were still reaching the frontlines.

Strangle was followed in March 1952 by Operation *Saturate*, a day and night interdiction campaign by UN fighter-bombers and night-flying B-26 Invaders against two-mile-long stretches of railway line. Although locally successful, it could not be extended effectively due to insufficient aircraft. In all, 330 FEAF aircraft (including 15 F9Fs) were lost to ground fire between August 18, 1951 and June 30, 1952, with 451 aircrew killed or captured.

In a final attempt to justify the interdiction strategy, which was beginning to lose favor with FEAF planners by early 1953, a massive onslaught by B-29s against a bridge complex between Sinanju and Yongmedong commenced on January 9, 1953. The next day, and for the following days, 300 fighter-bombers hit the bridges and surrounding AAA defenses (which were doubled during this time) and searchlight installations, causing total destruction. The enemy's solution was to build a 70-mile bypass around the area.

Increased supplies of Soviet AAA weaponry in 1951 allowed the KPA to establish up to 80 areas with substantial defenses that now routinely included early warning radar. Many had coordinated networks of heavier guns, radar, searchlights, and lighter weapons, although a number only had 37mm batteries and machine guns. The latter were concentrated along rail and supply lines. Storage areas and industrial sites were also defended, and Pyongyang, Sinuiju, the Sui-ho hydroelectric dam, and Manpojin, on the Yalu River, had substantial AAA defenses concentrated around them.

Whereas early in the war the relatively scarce AAA defenses tended to be scattered around the country in the hope of ambushing attacking aircraft, by 1952 more extensive resources allowed for massed batteries that were often placed very close to potential targets, with guns positioned only around 600ft apart. This eased the flak suppression flights' task, and it left many aircraft from large formations outside the guns' effective field-of-fire. As an alternative to hazardous flak suppression by CAS fighter flights, the US Army began to use its artillery to hit AAA sites along the frontline. Flight leaders could call in proximity-fuzed artillery fire on known AAA positions moments before they made their attack runs.

The aerial war of attrition against ground targets continued until the July 1953 armistice, by which point the communist expenditure on, and transport of, munitions had been reduced and UN interdiction had less of an effect because of a paucity of targets. As Col Richard Blanchfield (Senior Analyst and Assistant Director of the Strategic Assessment Center) put it, the war "began with a bang and ended with a whimper."

THE COMBATANTS

When the KPA invaded South Korea in June 1950, it assumed that the only aerial assets opposing the advance would likely be the handful of T-6 Texans flown by the RoKAF. Two months later, a USAF Air Intelligence report stated that North Korea's few AAA units had a "fairly high state of training and an aggressive attitude," but "cannot be considered as having a high deterrent value."

Although many of the troops serving were veterans of the war against Japan, they actually had little training in anti-aircraft tactics. US pilots saw soldiers standing in the open firing rifles at them while they made strafing passes. However, at low altitudes, basic infantry weapons could be destructive, as USAF B-26B, F-51D, and F-80C units discovered during early encounters with KPA soldiers in June–July 1950.

North Korea's air defenses expanded in response to USAF B-29 raids. In October 1950 it added a AAA regiment, ten more independent AAA battalions, and two AA machine gun companies. Guns were concentrated around Pyongyang and major transport routes near the frontline. From the summer of 1951, additional units protected hydroelectric plants, airfields, and bridges, and they were also placed on higher ground along likely B-29 approach routes. Their Soviet radar direction units were laboriously towed onto mountains, together with air defense command posts.

When low-altitude airfield attacks by F9Fs and other fighter-bombers began, 37mm batteries were repositioned on

their approach routes – some of these were also sited on higher ground, and many were constantly manned. A VF-51 division flying near Chosin power station in August 1951 was fired on from above by guns on surrounding hilltops, damaging Lt(jg) John Moore's Panther.

In 1950 the PVA possessed only 36 M1938 AAA weapons and around 100 automatic guns, with 18 12.7mm DShKM 1938s per infantry division, to assist in the defense of North Korea. Gen Peng Dehuai, leader of Chinese forces in Korea, asked Stalin for far more, but his existing batteries had to be arranged to provide limited defense. This meant that the 12.7mm DShKM 1938s were allocated to units in forward areas, while around 20 76.2mm M1938s, without radar guidance, were used in the rear.

Soviet intervention from December 1950 resulted in two MiG-15-equipped aviation divisions being based in China for operations over North Korea, followed by the 87th and 92nd Anti-aircraft Artillery Divisions and the 10th Searchlight Regiment. Each division consisted of five regiments with four batteries of six 37mm guns and four batteries of eight 85mm weapons, plus target acquisition and director radar units. They would defend the four Soviet airfields being built in the Antung area, as well as the bridges at Andong. High-altitude bombing raids by FEAF aircraft (principally B-29s) were initially intercepted by MiGs, after which heavy-caliber AAA took over. Both 85mm and 37mm weapons were used to deal with attacking aircraft flying at altitudes up to 10,000ft.

AAA units operating further east were usually manned by Chinese soldiers, or Soviet troops dressed in PVA cotton-quilt uniforms in order to disguise their presence in the war. One such soldier was Lt Nikolay Melteshinov, who was sent to Korea with a 76.2mm M1938-equipped AAA unit and issued with a Chinese uniform. He found that the guns were ineffective against US jets flying at 35,000ft, and also noted that steel helmets were vital for gun crews, as the falling shrapnel from their shells could be lethal. His unit taught Chinese gunners how to operate the M1938, and left them its weapons when it was withdrawn. Gunners soon realized that they were far more vulnerable than their own weapons, and could easily be replaced by standby crews if

M1938

Among the captured or obsolete AAA weaponry supplied to the KPA were M1938 76.2mm guns, which could fire a 14.5lb shell up to height of 30,500ft at the rate of 20 rounds per minute. Each gun required a commander and ten men to operate it.

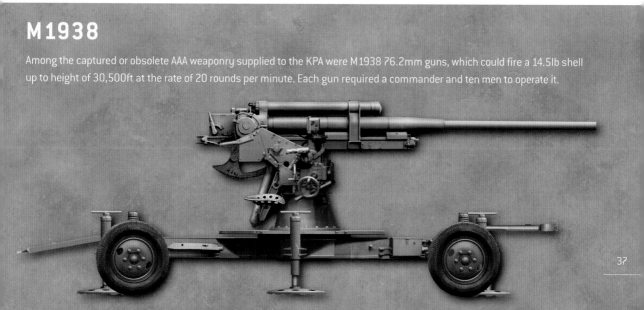

they were incapacitated by air attack. Nothing less than a direct hit by a bomb would eliminate both the gun and its crew.

In early September 1951, the Soviet Union's 87th Anti-aircraft Artillery Division moved into North Korea to cover airfields under construction at Taechon and Namsi, and they subsequently claimed 50 aircraft shot down between September 8 and the end of the year. They were particularly successful against low-flying propeller-driven aircraft thanks to the use of what Soviet gunners called "blocking fire." Such tactics could not be used when engaging high-flying targets, however. AAA could also prevent the rescue of downed pilots. For example, an attempt to recover Ens A. L. Riker of AD-3-equipped VA-923 from the Wonsan area on November 4, 1952 was frustrated by heavy groundfire, the pilot being posted as Missing in Action.

The training of Chinese troops destined for service manning AAA batteries in North Korea commenced in the months prior to the PVA's commitment to the conflict. In an attempt to allay Mao Zedong's fears that his army had insufficient anti-aircraft weapons, the PVA hastily established two air defense headquarters at Andong and Supung, near the border with North Korea, with Soviet forces providing the air power to defend both sites. Early warning and gun-laying radars were also supplied by the USSR, as were ground control interception radars – a particular worry to USAF bomber crews flying at night. Firing from their safe haven across the Yalu River, Chinese gunners scored their first success on October 15, 1950 when they shot down an F-51D – one of four Mustangs lost on operations that day.

UN aircraft flying in the area were regularly subjected to AAA from then on, and Soviet pilots patrolling the Yalu River were careful to avoid the gunners, as they had a reputation for shooting at any aircraft within range. Indeed, the batteries defending Andong shot down Capt Pasha Liuobovinkin's MiG as he returned to the base alone in March 1952. Nine months earlier, on June 23, 1951, Guards Lt Vladimir

M1940 (72-K)

The M1940 (72-K) 25mm AAA weapon equipped the KPA at the very start of the conflict in Korea, being fielded in both twin- and single-barrel (seen here) configuration. It was one of several Soviet designs (including the twin Model 94K and mobile ZSU-25) derived from the Swedish Bofors 25mm and 37mm weapons. This basic design also evolved into the widely used M1939 (61-K) 37mm AAA gun.

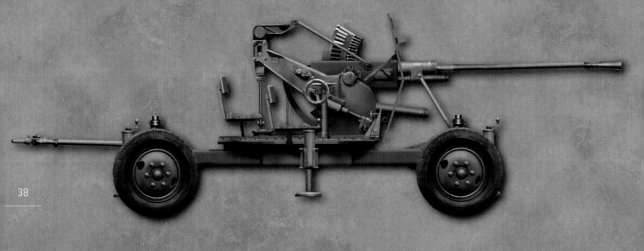

Negodiaev's MiG had fallen victim to North Korean gunners near Sonchon. Chinese air defense regiments in-theater never properly integrated with Soviet and North Korean units, and all three sometimes fired at MiGs. Problems with aircraft recognition were further exacerbated by the fact that Chinese Air Defense Force radars were mainly obsolete Soviet P-3 and P-3A early warning models with a range of just 200km.

In 1950 few 85mm KS-12 batteries had radar guidance. Accuracy was generally poor until April 5, 1951, when three out of four F-51s attacking a target at Sinmak were downed by gunfire. This was the first indication to the USAF that their opponents now had radar-controlled AAA weapons. The US Navy first knowingly encountered radar-controlled AAA five months later when, on September 4, the F9F of VF-51's Lt(jg) Ross Bramwell, flying from *Essex*, was hit near Haengsan in what was recorded as "the first burst seen in the area." Wingman Lt(jg) Tom Hayward recalled that, "We had scarcely entered the valley when the AAA lit up from all sides in extraordinary intensity. Bramwell was hit early. As he transmitted to us, his tail section burst into flames. I advised him to eject, but he struck the ground vertically and exploded." A second VF-51 Panther and its pilot were lost to AAA minutes later.

Occasionally, B-29s provided their own flak suppression with air-burst bombs, as during the September 30, 1952 attack on the Namsan-ni chemical plant. On at least one occasion B-29s also supplied flak suppression for US Navy aircraft. The rail junction city of Kowon in eastern Korea was a flak "hot spot" for F9Fs until ten B-29s hit it with 500lb proximity-fused bombs on October 8, 1952, followed up by low-level strafing by AD-4s and F9Fs. Only one AAA gun remained to fire at the US Navy aircraft following the Superfortress attack.

Eight months earlier, VF-111 pilots had noticed a marked increase in mobile 37mm weapons during their February 1952 rail cut missions, and their Panthers suffered far more damage from them than the ADs and F4Us flown by their fellow Naval Aviators from Air Task Group (ATG) 1 embarked in *Valley Forge*. Low-altitude approaches were favored, and where flak was light, these were made at 345mph at altitudes that allowed two feet for every pound of bomb weight (e.g. 500ft if 250lb bombs were carried). VF-111 pilots favored four 250lb bombs per aircraft per mission.

A further 26 AAA regiments in two more army groups were mobilized by the PVA in August 1951. M1939 guns were sited mainly around large railway marshaling yards and the most vital bridges. US fighter-bomber pilots attacking smaller bridges over the Yalu River in January 1951 often encountered nothing more than small-arms fire. Nevertheless, a lucky hit could still cripple a jet, so pilots generally stuck to the "one pass" rule to deny gunners a second chance.

By late 1952 additional heavy AAA sites had radar units, but in some locations searchlights were substituted to detect and track targets. By 1953 there were 500

Napalm canisters explode on North Korean trains. Mk 5 or Mk 12 fire-bombs were often used by land-based VMF-115 and VMF-311, while napalm-adapted Mk 66 practice bombs were briefly employed by *Leyte*'s CVG-3 in November 1950. However, the fire risk posed by napalm on carriers was deemed too great, and the weapon was quickly withdrawn from use. Two divisions of US Marine Corps Panthers would carry four bombs each, and some were used against AAA sites. (Hulton-Deutsch Collection/CORBIS/Corbis via Getty Images)

The ubiquitous DShK 1938 12.7mm heavy machine gun was a very effective anti-aircraft weapon, and examples used in the Korean War were built in China as the Type 54. Here, a weapon is manned by female gunners from the KPA in May 1953. (Keystone-France\Gamma-Rapho via Getty Images)

searchlight units in North Korea, many of them radar-controlled. Early warning radars and UN radio transmission interceptions usually warned the defenses of incoming attacks. Carrier-borne aircraft would be detected by pairs of search radar units on high ground, hidden in tree clusters. One picked up distant, high-flying formations and a second tracked closer, low-flying aircraft.

UN attacks on North Korea's hydroelectric production alarmed the country's leader, Kim Il Sung, who requested another ten AAA regiments to defend the dams. Stalin agreed to half that number, and insisted that the remaining five should come from China. Three regiments defended the Supung hydroelectric plant, while Stalin accelerated the formation and training of the People's Liberation Army Air Force. By the time UN aircraft attacked Supung in 1952, the gunners manning the AAA batteries were North Korean.

Whereas bombing from 10,000ft with several passes over the target had been possible in 1950, B-29s were forced by the proliferation of radar-controlled AAA to adopt high-altitude bombing as the war ground on. Dive-bombers were also more vulnerable as gunners fired an increasing number of high explosive rounds into their paths, affecting accuracy. Indeed, the circular error probable – the area of ground likely to be hit by half of the bombs dropped – increased from 75ft in 1951 to 219ft in 1953. This meant more re-attack missions were needed, giving the defenders some very predictable targets.

The instruction of KPA and PVA troops in the employment of Soviet equipment followed strict Red Army doctrine. Soviet artillery advisors congregated near Pyongyang and in the northwest of the country, sending problem-solving delegations to more remote areas. Their deployment of AAA relied on towing guns to new locations, usually at night, to meet unexpected threats. This was the case following the initial attacks on the Sui-ho hydroelectric dam in June 1952, when UN pilots experienced little in the way of AAA opposition. A re-attack several weeks later met fierce opposition, with the defenders having increased the number of heavy and automatic guns around the dam from 71 to 167.

Attackers tended to use the same target approach routes, so guns were arranged accordingly. They also habitually followed each other off-target in the same direction. *Oriskany's* Panther pilots noted in 1953 that, in order to disguise their locations, "many flak positions do not open fire until the attacking aircraft have passed over the target and are on their climb out". A *Princeton* After Action Report reminded pilots that "the dangers of affording enemy gunners advance information on one's position are obvious. On several occasions heavy flak concentrations were seen at the leader's break point [turn away from target] at about the same time the next plane would have been there, had he used the same break point."

The times of attacks at dawn and dusk were also predictable, as were ground signals like smoke rockets or colored fabric panel markers to call in CAS. UN pilots tried to avoid flak hot spots, and identifying them from the air was eased by light AA gunners' standard use of red tracers. Some of the most difficult flak suppression tasks were against well-camouflaged guns, often hidden in houses in civilian areas. Mobility of light AA weapons was such that CVG-5 mission planners decided in 1951 that, "The plotting of machine gun positions has proved useless. The guns are too easily moved, too hard to spot exactly by photo interpreters or pilot reports and too numerous to keep plotted."

The fighter-bombers had some success in hitting AAA units that were moving to new locations. Should this occur, gunners were told to be ready to fire back while on the move, or during a temporary halt. AAA convoys, including mobile radars and ammunition trucks, were protected in transit by 37mm or 40mm guns at the head, middle, and rear of the convoy.

Automatic and small arms fire caused most of the damage to Panthers flying "Cherokee" ground attack missions in early 1953 as the enemy moved ever-increasing numbers of heavy machine guns and 37mm weapons near the frontline. "Cherokee" attacks saw aircraft from four carriers, as well as land-based US Marine Corps air assets, target communist supply routes just north of the bomb line. The attacks were ordered by Vice-Adm Joseph "Jocko" Clark, commander of the Seventh Fleet. Clark was descended from the native American Cherokee tribe, hence the nickname given to the operations.

Between January 18 and February 8, 1953, VF-121 and VF-122 from *Oriskany* lost two jets to heavy-caliber AAA, and a further 12 Panthers suffered serious damage from small arms and automatic weapons as they made their low-altitude "Cherokee" attacks. On some occasions the flak was overwhelming due to the North Korean policy of concentrating light AAA defenses around selected target areas. On March 18, 1953

GORYUNOV SG-43

The Goryunov SG-43 7.62mm air-cooled machine gun dated from 1940, but it was still in use with several countries into the mid-1980s. Its simplicity and reliability made the SG-43 ideal for the harsh conditions of the Korean War, where it was widely used as both an infantry and AA weapon. Chinese license-produced versions known as the Type 53 predominated with the KPA.

M1939 (61-K)

The Soviet M1939 (61-K) 37mm gun was the AAA weapon most frequently encountered by F9F pilots during the Korean War, and it would also be fielded in large numbers by the North Vietnamese more than a decade later. Developed from the Bofors 25mm Model 1933, it entered service in 1939 and more than 20,000 examples were produced. The M1939 (61-K) was also license-built in China, North Korea, and Poland.

Oriskany's CVG-12 reported that when its aircraft "attacked supplies and military equipment behind the enemy's main line of resistance, extremely accurate and intense enemy AAA was encountered, despite the efforts of the flak-suppressing jets." On a second target, "damage assessment was hampered because of intense flak." The gunners' skill in setting up fake AAA sites also complicated assessment of their true strength.

By then, the US Navy's reconnaissance methods had become more refined, thus avoiding wasted anti-flak sorties against vacated AAA sites. As *Oriskany*'s Air Intelligence department recorded, "By checking daily photo coverage against the atlas, it was possible to eliminate duplicate reports of already designated targets. Instead of blindly reporting flak, it was possible to give recently abandoned flak positions an 'inactive' status, as well as reporting the existing AAA."

Pilots were also given 1:50,000 target "mosaic" images on which AAA positions were plotted so that they could "plan flak-free avenues of attack and withdrawal." AAA sites were marked as "heavy," "automatic," or "small arms, including machine guns." However, there were often many "unplotted" small-arms weapons to contend with. As the report noted, "Anti-aircraft fire in this theater, unlike German or Japanese AAA positions of World War II, is mobile. Positions pinpointed one day will or can be moved the following day."

Soviet and Chinese anti-aircraft tactics against low-flying targets relied on concentrated barrage fire from multiple weapons arranged in geometric patterns, usually a circle. Sometimes, gunners had time to take up well-planned defensive positions – a CVG-5 pilot reported that he "was hit by flak while making his run on a group of trucks surrounded by gun emplacements sending out intense and accurate AA fire."

The KPA set up "killer squads" of troops to fire small arms at any aircraft that appeared to be within range. Trainers instructed them to hold their fire until a fighter-bomber was pulling out from a diving attack or had passed over the target. One notorious 40mm site never fired until the aircraft had turned away from it, which meant spotting the gun was almost impossible.

Firing positions were set up on high ground near targets and supported by pilot distractions such as cables strung across valleys. Ens E. D. Jackson's Panther from VF-112 staggered back to *Philippine Sea* after a cable trap broke his canopy, wrecked the starboard tip tank and tore into the wing. As Lt Don Engen remembered it, near the Pusan enclave "You couldn't go half a mile without seeing a wing or a fuselage. Everybody was flying into wires, and the North Koreans were smart in stringing the wires up there. Wire strikes were a big issue."

Flak traps – a well-established way of luring aircraft into lethal situations – were common. Unserviceable or dummy vehicles were left in exposed positions as targets, surrounded with light anti-aircraft weapons and small-arms shooters, or a parachute would be draped in trees or dummy soldiers arranged around a fake tank. Sometimes rows of lights were set out to simulate a convoy of vehicles at night.

Essex's pilots estimated that flak was ten times more prevalent in late 1951 than in 1950, and in some areas, guns were twice as numerous as Japan's most intensive defenses in 1945. This made it increasingly difficult for US Navy mission planners to plot routes avoiding AAA "hot spots," so appropriate flak suppression ordnance had to be carried.

The AAA opposition was considerably reduced at night when the majority of transport was on the move. On dark, cold nights drivers had to occasionally use their headlights, and they usually kept their windows closed, blocking out aircraft noise. *Princeton* began night strikes in early 1951, and pilots were able to catch many locomotives and truck convoys in the open. Some pilots preferred these night "heckler" missions with less AAA and better targets, although bright moonlight still exposed them to ground fire. CVG-12 noted that "experience shows that the enemy's AAA control systems are rarely effective at night." Pairs of "hecklers," usually F4U-5Ns or AD-4Ns, were typically launched, although no carrier was designated for full night operations. F9F units were seldom scheduled for night operations.

Occasionally, when radar was unavailable for the gunners, MiG-15s were sent up to pace attacking bombers, reporting their altitude and heading to the AAA batteries. For frequently attacked sites such as the Sui-ho hydroelectric dam or Sinanju bridge complex, the KPA studied the attack formations' usual approach routes and located guns along them, rather than at the target. Fighter-bombers varied their approaches and attacked from multiple directions to confuse the gunners. F9F pilots often found that M1939 (61-K) 37mm fire was the most difficult to avoid at low altitude since the gunners could more easily track their target and use the gun's rapid rate of fire to bracket them.

JETS ON DECKS

Panther pilots had no two-seat F9Fs for training, and most got their jet experience on Lockheed TV-1s – 50 F-80Cs acquired in 1949. For air-to-air preparation, the assumption made by Cdr Ralph Weymouth, CO of CVG-11 (embarked in *Philippine Sea* in 1950–51), was that "due to the tremendous speeds, the firing time allowed would restrict tactics to a single pass and breakaway for each airplane in a division, and then a complete repositioning for a second attack." In practice, Weymouth's F9F pilots from VF-111 and VF-112 found that situations resembling traditional dogfights were actually more likely during their five MiG-15 encounters in November 1950 because of the jets' similar speeds. Pilots performed "scissors" maneuvers during high-speed turning and diving engagements.

Many of the early F9F squadrons included experienced fighter pilots who had seen combat in World War II. One such Naval Aviator was veteran FM-2 Wildcat pilot Lt Cdr Tom Amen, who was given command of VF-111 in February 1950. Flying jets from the 1940s Essex-class carriers was a risky business, and during the Korean War such a vessel was likely to lose a tenth of its aircrew on a deployment, which could last up to eight months.

The US Navy's mid-1947 Project 27A had seen its Essex-class carriers, starting with *Oriskany*, modified for post-war operations through the fitment of more powerful H-8 hydraulic catapults, jet blast deflectors, and Mk V arresting gear to allow them to operate jets at heavier weights. For the F9F's early cruises, there were no blast shields to protect deck crew and aircraft while pilots wound up the engines of their Panthers to take-off power. Even on a Project 27A carrier, launching a bombed-up F9F-2B was still only marginally feasible. *Princeton* did find an alternative use for the jets' "hot breath" – in the winter of 1951 Panthers were used "for the initial removal of snow" from the flightdeck. They also proved "most effective in drying the deck."

Powering up an F9F's engine required an external electrical starter unit, which generated ten percent rpm. Moving the throttle to the "start" position opened the high-pressure fuel cock and supplied electrical power to the igniter, which normally lit the engine within 30 seconds. Spool-up to maximum power took 12 seconds. With 20 percent power and 400°C tailpipe temperature, the throttle was moved to the idle position, with 28 percent rpm.

Taxiing out required 51 percent rpm, with steering supplied by the toe brakes. Once in the air, pilots generally found that the Panther was vice-free to handle, even with ordnance aboard. Compared with the view forward from a piston-engined fighter, it was easy to see the landing signals officer (LSO, nicknamed "paddles") guiding the Panther onto the flightdeck. The airframe was stressed for +7.5g and -3g up to 20,000ft and 480mph. In service, Panthers proved to be reliable and straightforward to maintain. For the second half of 1950, US Navy F9F squadrons achieved 96 percent availability rates in combat conditions.

Carrier launching required a bridle attached behind the nose wheel and a frangible hold-back bar fitted aft of the main landing gear. With a careful eye on the wind-over-deck readings on a hand-held anemometer, the carrier air group's catapult officer adjusted the aircraft's take-off weight by ordering the progressive removal of bombs or rockets from under its wings until it reached a weight at which it could achieve the correct speed at the end of the World War II-vintage H4B

Korea presented some extreme winter operating conditions both on land and at sea. Panthers with folded wings had to be carefully chained down on icy flightdecks in high winds, as they could easily skid around. (US Navy)

catapult. Even then, the jet was likely to sink towards the sea as it left the flightdeck, with its stall-warning "stick shaker" device in panic mode. If a pilot then pulled up too sharply he would stall, so he had to let the aircraft accelerate to a safe flight speed.

Canopies were slid back for take-off to facilitate a quick exit in the water. Sometimes the pilot could be picked up by the rescue helicopter, although the ditched F9F could just as easily be "run over" by the ship before he could escape. Lt Wayne Cheal's Panther – *Valley Forge*'s first loss during its 1950 cruise – hit the water on May 21 and the ship's bow pushed against the floating jet as Cheal stood up in his cockpit. He swam clear and was picked up. Three years later, on July 26, 1953, the very last Panther lost during the Korean War suffered a "cold shot" off *Boxer* and hit the sea ahead of the carrier. Ens Tom Ledford of VF-151 failed to extricate himself from the F9F-2 before it sank with him trapped inside the cockpit.

In July 1950's high heat and low winds, *Valley Forge* (nicknamed the "Happy Valley") had to cancel 40 percent of its Panther launches, as the jet needed at least 33 knots of wind over the deck. The marginal launch conditions meant that for many missions only 20mm armament could be carried. Even three knots of windspeed over the deck could make the difference between a fully fueled Panther launching with six rockets and 33 knots of wind over the deck, or no external ordnance with only 30 knots of wind. Carrier-launched Panthers flying from Essex-class vessels with hydraulic catapults were unable to carry bombs until April 1951, when VF-191 launched its F9F-2Bs from *Princeton* for a bridge attack with four 250lb and two 100lb bombs apiece.

Recovery to the Essex-class straight deck carriers required extreme accuracy and complete trust in the LSO, and the "paddles" with which he indicated whether a jet was too high, too low, on speed, etc. If the tailhook did not catch an arresting wire, or bounced over them all, a pilot had to run into the Davis barrier – a strong nylon net that caught the nosewheel and also raised a thick wire cable that engaged the main gear legs and stopped the aircraft. Failing that, he would run on into a 12-ft nylon palisade barrier that wrapped around the wings to prevent the aircraft from crashing into the mass of parked aircraft on the foredeck area. Even that sometimes failed to prevent a major collision. On September 29, 1950, during VF-111's first combat cruise embarked in *Philippine Sea*, Ens J. Omvig's F9F-2 surged through all the barriers, seriously injuring two deck crew and damaging 12 aircraft, five of them badly. Omvig emerged from the wreckage of his Panther uninjured.

Some Essex-class ships had a homing beacon to assist pilots on their return, but finding a carrier in poor weather conditions or darkness remained a challenge.

COMBAT MISSIONS

Most missions lasted around 1.5 hours, with a two hours maximum for carrier-based Panthers, allowing a minimal 133 gallons reserve. The majority of the sorties flown were armed reconnaissance, undertaken at altitudes of 1,000–3,000ft, where light anti-aircraft and small-arms fire were constant hazards. Usually, two-aircraft sections, or four-jet divisions with two "high" and two "low" F9Fs, flew along a pre-planned railway line or road route at close quarters to see below the camouflage that frequently disguised valuable targets during daylight hours. The enemy became skilful at hiding trucks or supplies in the time it took for a Panther pilot to turn back after spotting a target, arm his guns, and set up an attack run.

Trains would be hidden in tunnels by day, where attempts to launch bombs or fire 20mm rounds into the entrance seldom had much effect. In the exception to this rule, Ens Allen Hill and a VF-112 wingman on a "road recce" mission in late 1950 successfully attacked a troop and ammunition train with 6.5in. anti-tank aircraft rockets (ATARs) as it entered a short tunnel, causing a massive secondary explosion. CVG-5 F9F pilots reported in 1950–51 that, "the Reds are using trains and tunnel entrances as flak traps. The train waits just outside the tunnel. When the pilot makes his [attack] run, the train scoots into the tunnel for protection, and AA batteries near the mouth of the tunnel get an excellent shot at him."

Strike missions, with an approach to the target at 10,000–20,000ft and weapons delivery in a 35- to 50-degree dive, allowed one run at a well-defended target, and more if defenses were light. More often F9Fs would be flying as flak suppressors for piston-engined strike aircraft, or occasionally as target markers for the strike.

For CAP sorties, flown without external ordnance, Panthers maintained 90-minute CAP stations offshore from the target area at around 20,000ft. On TARCAPs the jets would be nearer to MiG threats from Manchurian bases, flying at 20,000ft in figure-eight patterns along the North Korean border.

After launching for a ground attack mission, a division of Panthers would rendezvous and visually inspect each other's rockets or bombs to check that arming wires were not loosened by whipping motions in high-speed flight. Gunsights were switched on, giving their gyros time to stabilize, and later in the flight guns were test-fired. For ground attack, the 20mm guns were usually the primary weapon due to their accuracy, but 5in. HVARs could be deadly. They were usually launched at around 1,500ft from the target in a 35-degree dive to avoid debris damage from exploding rockets. Strafing could involve lower dive angles.

During VF-111's first deployment one pilot demonstrated the Panther's toughness when he followed his HVARs too closely to the target and flew close to their explosion. Although he managed to land back on board *Philippine Sea*, shrapnel damage wrote off his Panther.

There were plenty of hazards awaiting an F9F division once it went "feet dry" over land apart from those created by the enemy. Mountainous terrain, severe weather, and sometimes unreliable ground control approach provisions took many lives. On September 10, 1952, F9Fs from VMF-115 were returning to K-3 Pohang but six were diverted to K-2 Taegu and flew into a 4,000ft mountain obscured by thick fog. There

In April 1952 VMF-115 began exchanging its F9F-4s for ex-US Navy F9F-2s with fewer hours on their airframes. The unit flew a mixed force of nine "Dash-2s" and 14 "Dash-4s" during 1952–53 until sufficient F9F-5s were available to re-equip VMF-115 in its entirety in late April 1953. These jets, seen at K-13 Suwon in the early spring of 1952, are about to fly their second mission of the day, which will end with their recovery at their home base of K-3 Pohang. (US Marine Corps)

were no survivors. Another pilot returning to the base on instruments in his F9F-5 had to make a second approach in very low clouds, misjudged his climb-out and hit a 3,000ft mountain near K-3 Pohang at high speed.

As the war progressed, an increasing number of US Naval and US Marine Corps Reservists made up the numbers in operational squadrons or deployed in complete units that had been called to active duty. An example of the latter was VF-721, which had been mobilized on July 20, 1950 and assigned to CVG-101. The latter duly embarked in *Boxer* in March of the following year and sailed for Korea.

By November 1951 US Naval Reserve aviators were flying three-quarters of the carrier-borne strikes, while 48 percent of the pilots in the 1st Marine Air Wing (MAW), which had been involved in the conflict in Korea since July 1950, were "weekend warriors" posted in from Reserve units based in the US. Among the latter was 33-year-old Major League Baseball star Capt Ted Williams, who was recalled to duty in January 1952 and joined VMF-311 in February

Capt Ted Williams mounts the extending step and three spring-loaded indents in the fuselage side to enter the cockpit of his Panther. Williams interrupted his $100,000-a-year job with the Boston Red Sox Major League Baseball team against a background of protest that his recall to active service was intended to provide publicity for the US Marine Corps. He flew with VMF-311 in-theater. (US Marine Corps)

of the following year at K-3 Pohang when it began to run short of pilots. Future astronaut Maj John Glenn was posted in 12 days later. Pohang was a busy base in 1953 – on Glenn's first day he saw 28 F9F sorties launched in groups of four or eight by VMF-311, with another 20 generated by VMF-115.

Williams' F9F-5 was hit by small-arms fire on several missions, and on 16 February its hydraulics were damaged by bullets or shrapnel during a low-altitude bomb-drop, forcing him to crash-land the burning jet at the USAF's K-13 Suwon airfield at 225mph. He escaped with minor injuries after a 5,000ft slide down the concrete runway – fortunately, the longest in Korea. The entire underside of the jet was scraped away.

Conditions for F9F maintainers at Pohang and most other bases in Korea were extremely primitive. There were no hangars for repairs and deep maintenance at K-3, despite the dreadful winter weather. A land-based Panther squadron had 12 jets, each with a plane captain in charge of maintenance, supervised by a line chief. Pilots seldom flew the same aircraft regularly.

Occasionally, all available jets from VMF-311 and VMF-115 shared the same interdiction target, expending formidable amounts of ordnance. On April 4, 1953, a joint strike by 24 F9F-5s dropped eight 500lb bombs on several targets and 16 260lb

VMF-311's Capt Ted Williams was attacking targets on Highway 1 south of Pyongyang on February 16, 1953 when his F9F-5 (BuNo 126109) was hit by ground fire or shrapnel and burst into flames. Needing to land as soon as possible, Williams nursed his fighter back to K-13 Suwon, where he bellied it in on fire. The jet skidded along the tarmac for almost a mile, with sparks flying from it. When the Panther finally came to a halt, the nose promptly caught fire, threatening the cockpit. Williams duly blew off the canopy, struggled out, and limped away. (US Marine Corps)

fragmentation bombs for flak suppression. They also fired 42 ATARs and 450 rounds of 20mm ammunition. The Panthers met substantial heavy and automatic AAA over one target but sustained no damage.

Nevertheless, as VMF-311's historian noted, "Enemy anti-aircraft fire kept the maintenance section jumping during June [1953] as 15 jets returned from missions with battle damage. This was readily accepted, however, by squadron personnel, since no planes were lost and no pilots were missing or injured." Sadly, the gunners accounted for three Panthers (with a fourth downed by the explosion of one of the F9Fs hit by AAA) and two pilots on July 17. These were the last US Marine Corps Panthers lost during the conflict in Korea.

Strafing remained a key form of attack for F9F units through to war's end – on one 24-aircraft strike in early 1953, Panthers expended 4,150 20mm rounds. Buildings, storage caves, ammunition dumps, mortar positions, and troop concentrations were regular targets. F9F pilots often commented on the lack of effective AAA and small-arms fire during their missions along the "bomb line" in the final months of the conflict, describing it as "meager" or "inaccurate." In fact, VMF-311 survived June 1953 without loss or serious damage to any aircraft apart from Maj Glenn's, which had a flak hole punched through the tail.

Glenn, the first American astronaut to orbit the earth, gained a reputation for being both a "bridge buster" and a "flak magnet" during his 63 missions with VMF-311. His aircraft was hit 12 times by AAA. Glenn was considered to be an aggressive pilot who would conduct attacks below "safe" altitudes. On one CAS mission he was hit by an 85mm round that shot three feet off of his wing and removed a napalm tank, but he still managed to recover to Pohang. A confrontation with a 37mm AAA site on June 1, 1953 left him exposed to another 37mm AAA site that scored a hit and made his F9F dive towards a paddy field. Glenn just managed to pull up and coax the Panther home. Capt Ted Williams was Glenn's wingman for around 12 missions.

COMBAT

For the F9F's first combat deployment, with VF-51 and VF-53 in CVG-5 embarked in *Valley Forge*, 28 Panthers and 40 pilots were available to TF 77. The units' preparation for combat was minimal as Lt Don Engen recalled. "In terms of tactics, We had the 'Thach weave' and the 'fluid four'. We knew we had something that nobody had had before which was speed and power, so we tried to devise tactics to use these. Our only 'targets', however, prior to entering combat were either prop airplanes from the air group or other Panthers. We were always attacking somebody who had either less or equal performance to us.

"Once on cruise, we kept running into the mindset where senior personnel within the ship's company were afraid of us flying in case we could not get back aboard. This meant we were actually flying just four hours a month, and that's dangerous when conducting operations at sea."

CVG-5 entered combat on July 3 when it attacked airfields around Pyongyang in conjunction with Fleet Air Arm Fireflies and Seafires from *Triumph*. Twenty-eight AD-4 Skyraiders (from VA-55) and F4U Corsairs (from VF-53 and VF-54) took part, while the Panther squadrons weighed in with their first combat sorties led by the Commander Air Group (CAG), Cdr Harvey Lanham, with Lt Engen as his section leader. The latter recalled, "Aside from CAG Lanham's four jets, [Lt Cdr] Dave Pollock [CO of VF-51] had four airplanes and so did [Lt Cdr] Bill Lamb [CO of VF-52]. It was a wild melée. There were lots of targets, and we did the first pre-emptive strike in Korea. Although I was chasing a Yak and I just about had him boresighted, Harvey called me back."

The F9F pilots' main purpose that day was to strafe enemy aircraft on several airfields and fend off any aerial opposition. Seventeen NKPAF aircraft were destroyed in revetments on the ground in two attacks on the 3rd and in follow-up raids on July 4. Lt Engen flew F9F-3s BuNos 123069 and 123023, and his logbook for the 3rd

F9F-5 PANTHER GUN ARMAMENT

1. Detachable nose cone
2. Gun ports and blast shields
3. Forward gun support
4. AN/ARN-6 radio compass mounting
5. Electronics units
6. Left M3 20mm cannon
7. Left 20mm ammunition box
8. Right 20mm ammunition box
9. Electrical leads
10. Battery
11. Left ammunition tracks
12. Lower nose compartment
13. Mk 6 Mod 0 gun/weapons sight
14. Bulletproof windshield
15. Grumman ejection seat
16. Canopy slide mechanism
17. Air brakes (retracted)
18. Boarding ladder (retracted)
19. Forward armor plating
20. Aft seatback armor plating

includes the brief entries "Sweep on Pyongyang. 1 Yak and 1 DC-3" for the morning mission and "1 Yak and 5 freight cars" in the afternoon. The squadron would fly 436 fighter sweeps during its 1950 war cruise.

The US Navy's first aerial success with jets also came on July 3. VF-51's Lt(jg) Leonard H. Plog and his wingman were strafing an airfield when they saw a Yak-9P piston-engined fighter taking off. When Plog moved in for a stern attack as the Yak climbed to 350ft, another Yak-9P made an unsuccessful firing pass at him from his left side. A third Yak-9P then appeared and moved in on CAG Lanham and his wingman, Lt Bill Gormley. Ens "Little" Ed Brown quickly closed in on the Yak and severed its tail section with 20mm fire from very short range, while Plog, in F9F-3

BuNo 123071, pursued his target "on the deck" and shot the right wing off the NKPAF fighter with a short burst of 20mm fire. As Lt Engen pointed out:

> Those four 20s were like a can opener. You loaded them with armor-piercing tracer, HEI [high explosive incendiary] and antipersonnel rounds. That combination could blow up locomotives and sink ships. When the four 20s hit in a focus point, things happened.

The pilots flew fairly flat strafing runs, giving them a longer time to sight their targets. They also discovered that the F9F yawed at high speed, spoiling accurate strafing. Improvements came from using the speed brakes to slow down, but this reduced hydraulic pressure and the guns stopped firing.

Brown and Plog used up their ammunition on aircraft hidden in haystacks, vehicles, the control tower, and a fuel dump, returning in the afternoon for another strike. Plog reported that "anti-aircraft fire was minimal on both strikes." He noticed that the gunners took a long time to adjust to the higher speeds of the unfamiliar jets, so that their shells were detonating up to 1,500ft behind them.

These early "group grope" missions established a routine that applied for the rest of the war, but required careful timing. Attack squadron Skyraiders and Corsairs left the carrier first, followed by the jets, which caught them up just before the target, provided cover over it, and protected their withdrawal. The F9Fs' shorter endurance limited the time ADs and F4Us could spend attacking their targets.

Although the Panther's quartet of 20mm cannon were at first the aircraft's only weapon, they could be extremely effective for both flak suppression and the destruction of ground targets. On VF-191's first combat cruise, embarked in *Princeton*, two jets hit K-27 Yonpo airfield on December 21, 1950. Post-strike assessment reported "70 cases of rockets were exploded by strafing. One gun emplacement was damaged. Strafing caused 14 fires among oil and gas drums." The following day, former Blue Angels pilot Lt J. H. Robcke led a section of F9F-2s to a village, where "50 to 60 drums of oil were strafed and destroyed."

For the first few months of operations over Korea, TF 77's carrier-based aircraft primarily flew armed reconnaissance sorties as CVG-5 pioneered the use of jets operating alongside propeller-driven aircraft. Eventually, F9Fs would range from the east coast north of the town of Hamhung – where VF-23's flak-suppressing Panthers would silence 85mm guns at marshaling yards on August 3, 1952 – to Kwangju, on the western side of North Korea, and north to Namwon and Kaesong.

Some missions could be pre-planned, but often pilots were given routes and told to find likely targets. Manhandling two or three large 1:250,000 L-552 maps in the cockpit in fast, low-altitude flight became a daily challenge. Known flak sites were marked on the L-552s. Attacks on fixed sites like airfields, bridges, and power stations could be briefed in detail, but pilots also strafed targets of opportunity, including vehicles, trains (the weight of fire from four 20mm cannon could explode a locomotive's boiler), boats, troop concentrations, and even ammunition-bearing camel caravans.

The KPA soon became adept at using natural terrain and foliage to camouflage its parked up vehicles and supplies during the hours of daylight. Pilots had to fly as low as possible to see beneath such disguises, risking AAA at close quarters or possibly striking high ground while attempting to avoid gunfire.

F9F-2B BuNo 123443 from VF-112 floats on the water following an unsuccessful launch from *Philippine Sea* off Mokpo-Kwang-Ju on August 7, 1950. Its pilot, Cdr Ralph Weymouth (CAG of CVG-11), can be seen standing in the cockpit of his jet awaiting rescue. This aircraft, which had suffered an engine failure seconds after departing its carrier, was the first of three Panthers lost during the deployment. (US Navy)

Armed reconnaissance missions often yielded outstanding results in the early months of the war, when AAA defenses were light. For example, seven VF-51 Panthers were on a mission along the eastern Korean coast on July 18, 1950 when they "discovered" the Wonsan oil refining plant, capable of producing 500 gallons of petroleum daily. Later that same day, a TF 77 strike group reduced it to rubble.

Lt Don Engen flew some of the first road reconnaissance missions undertaken by Panthers. "We would send two F9Fs along a road for 150 miles, two more F9Fs on another road and two to cover a rail line. With the elimination of the NKPAF, there was no air opposition. We had the skies all to ourselves. We set about trying to interdict transportation to the maximum extent. Once we finished with the airplanes on their airfields, we went after ships, then trains. We were always going after trains."

Sections of F9Fs flew with one aircraft at an altitude of 50–100ft and a second following higher so that it could immediately attack targets found by the "low" jet. Lt Engen's regular wingman, Ens John Nyhuis, became the first F9F pilot to fall victim to ground fire when, on August 12, 1950, his jet was hit by 40mm AAA while the pair were strafing a train. The Panther crashed shortly thereafter, and no trace of Nyhuis was ever found.

B-26 and B-29 bombers destroyed many bridges and stretches of railway track, but the resourceful KPA soon bridged gaps in the supply lines by using human porters, often Chinese conscripts. Panthers and other fighter-bombers were tasked with trying to interdict such stretches of the logistical network with armed reconnaissance sorties. During its first fortnight of action, CVG-5 flew nearly 600 sorties – many of them against supply lines.

CVG-5 had the dubious distinction of suffering the first ditching by a US Navy jet involved in Korean War operations when an F9F-3 from VF-51 had a "cold shot" (insufficient pressure in the catapult to achieve a safe launch speed) on July 16, 1950. The Panther's wingtip and undercarriage clipped the water, cartwheeling the jet to an abrupt halt. The stunned pilot was quickly rescued by the carrier's HO3S-1 plane guard helicopter. During the third "cold shot" of the cruise, on August 12, the VF-51 pilot involved was able to raise his gear before the jet "skimmed" into the sea. He duly climbed out while the F9F remained afloat.

Five days earlier, *Philippine Sea*, which had only been on station for 48 hours, also lost an F9F-2B (from VF-112) when it suffered an engine failure moments after launching. Its pilot, CVG-11 CAG Cdr Weymouth, was quickly rescued. The ordnance-carrying capabilities of CVG-11's two F9F-2B squadrons were urgently needed to help save embattled UN forces trapped in a small area around Pusan.

Traveling mostly at night, communist troops had advanced southward totally undetected until they were finally spotted by US Navy photo-reconnaissance aircraft attempting to complete their flanking movement. To prevent a "Dunkirk" withdrawal, or worse, FEAF aircraft attacked roads leading into the area to paralyze the enemy supply lines. *Valley Forge* launched two divisions of F9Fs four times daily, although its efforts were hampered by inadequate tactical air control.

During the attempts in November 1950 to restrain the Chinese advance into South Korea, TF 77 aircraft from three carriers – *Valley Forge*, *Philippine Sea*, and *Leyte* – assisted USAF attacks on the five Yalu bridges, since they had been successful in destroying smaller bridges in the south during the brief North Korean occupation. Panther divisions provided top cover. Attackers could not enter Manchurian air space or damage the Manchurian ends of the bridges over the Yalu. Chinese AAA firing at them from Manchuria was also immune from counterattack, including guns that had been moved by the KPA to safety on the Manchurian side of the Yalu. The gunners were so confident of their immunity that they did not camouflage their weapons.

The difficulty of this task was well understood by senior officers. Vice-Adm C. Turner Joy remarked that, "The hazards of employing aircraft in precision attacks on small targets protected by intense, well-directed anti-aircraft fire which cannot be attacked, as well as by enemy planes flying in the haven of neutral territory, are tremendous."

Lt Cdr William R. Pittman, commanding VF-53's flak-suppressing Corsairs embarked in *Valley Forge*, flew a number of early missions against bridges in late 1950. He observed that, "Our jets [F9F-3s from VF-52] usually took up a position ahead and well above us. At this stage of the war, we propeller pilots were increasingly thankful (and not a little envious) of the jets. They were our only protection against the MiGs."

On November 8 Sinuiju was bombed by B-29s, while 300 fighters spent the morning on flak suppression with guns, rockets, and napalm. Between November 9

A typical TF 77 carrier strike would see piston-engined F4Us and ADs launch well in advance of their faster, flak-suppressing F9F escorts. Nevertheless, the Panthers would still arrive over the target moments before the Corsairs and Skyraiders, thus offering crucial flak suppression.

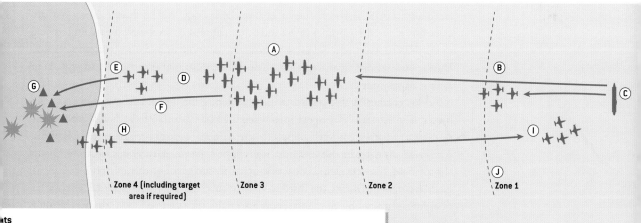

Zone 4 (including target area if required)   Zone 3   Zone 2   Zone 1

ts
Strike force aircraft – several flights of F4U Corsairs and AD Skyraiders.
F9Fs leaving the carrier.
Carrier at 200 miles from target.
Strike force aircraft and escort meet at target.
F9Fs dive from 20,000ft, firing 20mm cannon, then drop 260lb fragmentation bombs from 3,000ft, pulling out at 6g, and climbing away at a 45-degree angle.
Strike force flights dive from 12,000ft to attack with bombs and rockets.
Communist anti-aircraft defenses.
F9Fs leaving the target.
In good visibility, descent to the carrier begins at Mach 0.7.
Zones in which extra escort flights could be provided if necessary.

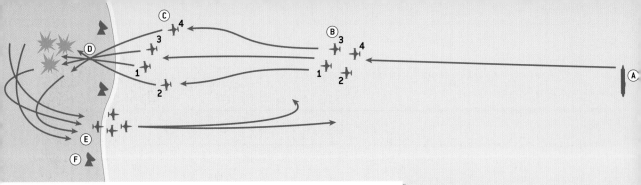

F9F-only strikes against pre-briefed targets usually involved flights of four Panthers flying in two-aircraft sections.

and 21, carrier-based aircraft flew 593 sorties, dropping 232 tons of bombs, but the massive bridge structures were only damaged. Towards the end of this phase of the prolonged bridge campaign the Yalu froze over and communist traffic could cross the river without having to use the bridges. After November 29 the US Navy aircraft reverted to flying CAS missions for US Marine Corps units retreating to Hungnam.

TF 77 aircraft were allowed to conduct interdiction missions in eastern North Korea from late January 1951. Rail routes and bridges were attacked daily to deter repairs, and AAA opposition was severe. Lt Cdr Paul Gray, commander of AD-4-equipped VF-54 embarked in *Essex*, recalled that his aircraft rarely returned without some AAA damage.

Attacks on the 600ft-long bridge built 60ft above "Carlson's Canyon" near Kilchu, detected by *Princeton*'s photo-reconnaissance aircraft in March, demonstrated the determination of both sides. Supported by five massive concrete piers and six steel spans, with two tunnels, the bridge was a vital component in the eastern rail network, linking three lines originating in Manchuria. The area had at least 100 AAA sites.

Attacks on March 3 and 7, led by Lt Cdr Harold Carlson's VA-195, also embarked in *Princeton*, caused severe damage. The wooden beams that were used to repair the bridge were destroyed with napalm on March 15. Despite a B-29 attack with anti-personnel bombs shortly thereafter, the bridge was in limited use again by April 2. TF 77's whole might was focused on the structure on April 3 and 4, totally destroying it. Communist forces soon built a detour rail route, avoiding the canyon.

These missions in "Carlson's Canyon" became the subject of the book and film *The Bridges at Toko-Ri*, and the specific attack covered in both was based on a bridge-bombing operation on December 12, 1951, led by Lt Cdr Gray of VF-54. VF-51's Panthers and VF-172's Banshees, also embarked in *Essex* as part of CVG-5, formed the fighter components, facing 56 AAA guns (mostly 37mm but including some 100mm weapons) controlled by 11 radars.

Although unable to carry the heavy ordnance loads routinely slung under the wings of the Skyraider and Corsair, F9F-2Bs could be laden down with up to 1,200lbs of bombs if a particularly strong wind was blowing over the bow of the carrier. Such conditions were present on April 2, 1951, when a pair of Panthers from VF-191 launched from *Princeton* with two 250lb GP bombs fuzed for explosion on contact, two 250lb GP bombs with eight- to 15-second delay fuzes and two 100lb GP bombs.

The jets were flown by Lt Cdr Ben Riley and Lt Ray Hawkins, who each dropped four 250lb bombs and two 100 lb GP bombs on a Songjin railway bridge. The latter had already been destroyed and rebuilt, so the attack was made at very low altitude in an attempt to secure its final destruction. One F9F-2B was badly damaged by its own bomb shrapnel as a result.

Panther pilots from VF-721 attend a mission briefing in their squadron ready room on board *Boxer* during the ship's 1951 combat cruise. The briefing was followed by a dash up to the flightdeck, where the Naval Aviators manned their awaiting F9Fs. (US Navy)

When Panthers dived at 500mph to release bombs at 3,000ft, their pull-out from an angle of 45 degrees would take them down to 1,500–2,000ft – well within range of light AAA. Their aircraft would also risk suffering shrapnel damage from their own bombs if they were fused to explode on impact. Accuracy was compromised by bombing from higher altitudes. US Marine Corps squadron VMF-115 evolved tactics that included a 35–40 degree dive with airbrakes extended and the engine throttled back to 75 percent power. Delayed-action bombs were dropped at 1,800ft, followed by a high-g pull out at maximum power and hard "jinking" to avoid flak. Such tactics balanced bombing accuracy against exposure to AAA. Previously, VMF-115 had attacked targets in a 20-degree dive so as to reduce the tendency for the F9F to sink over the target in a high-g pull-out.

The assault on the rail network included attempts to seal off tunnels, averaging 1,200ft in length, by bombing. Rarely, fighter-bomber pilots could lob bombs into tunnel mouths, causing partial collapses or destruction of a sheltering train. The mountainous eastern side of the country had 1,140 miles of track, 956 bridges, and 231 tunnels, all of which were repeatedly damaged by TF 77. This in turn forced the communists to use the western network instead, or rely on trucks by night.

Lt Don Engen recalled attempting to destroy a train on the eastern network. "I set his coal car on fire but he still had power and entered a tunnel where I could not get him. I'm sitting there watching, and pretty soon smoke emerged from both ends of the tunnel. He probably couldn't stand it, and he came out of the tunnel like a shot, and I hit him again. He went into another tunnel and he ran me out of gas."

The incessant repair effort by the massive labor force in North Korea seemed to negate all the US Navy pilots' achievements.

SUPPRESSING FLAK

Flak suppression – a regular mission by 1951 – was regarded as one of the most demanding, as it required precise planning and timing to coordinate the attacks and minimize exposure to enemy fire. Pilots tasked with this mission supported bomb-runs by "prop" flights, with the faster Panthers arriving moments before the piston-engined aircraft and blasting AAA sites with 20mm cannon fire, time-delayed fragmentation bombs, and rockets. Ideally, the gunners would be silenced while the strike aircraft hit the target. Some pilots hoped gunners would just take cover, but the latter's strict codes of discipline and loyalty seldom allowed this degree of self-preservation.

CVG-19's tactics from 1952, which were similar to others, were adapted to the perceived threat. "In low-density flak areas, bombing was done by divisions in rotation. Each plane in the division made a glide-bombing run from 6,000–8,000ft, released at 2,500–3,000ft and recovered at 1,500ft. One division always stayed on top to spot for possible flak opposition and the drops of the division bombing. Directions of dive and recovery were varied. For missions in high-density flak areas, coordinated attacks were made using the VF [fighter] aircraft for flak suppression. Flights were always briefed as to the direction of [bombing] run, retirement, and rendezvous, and all were varied. Out-of-the-sun runs were favored."

In strikes on Anbyon-up on August 8, 1952, F9Fs, ADs, and F4Us all made coordinated flak suppression and strike runs, and 12 days later, F4Us alone took on the 85mm and 100mm sites with VT-fuzed 1,000lb GP bombs, meeting exceptionally heavy AAA. Five months earlier, VF-51's CO, Cdr George Duncan, had used two coordinated divisions, one approaching from the north and a second from the west, in a March 9, 1952 "Cherokee" flak suppression mission.

By August 1952, half of the missions being flown from *Essex* by ATG-2's two F9F-2 squadrons (VF-23 and VF-821) were flak suppression due to the "major build-up of flak throughout the primary target areas of North Korea." They developed two types of attack, with approaches at 15,000–20,000ft. "In one, all the jets go in before the prop aircraft, and in the other, 50 percent of the jets go in first, with the remaining jets coming in with the last of the prop aircraft. Timing and location of the flak are the keys to success in this mission. Too often, the flak has not been pinpointed, with the result that area strafing and bombing must be used. This is inefficient, and will usually keep the gunners' heads down for only short periods of time. The prop aircraft should be well in their dive when the jets pull out. On a few occasions where there was a considerable lag between the jet and prop attacks, the flak was of heavier intensity and more accurate."

"Dueling" with AAA or making multiple target runs greatly increased the risks of being shot down, so they were generally avoided. From June 1952, USAF pilots were limited to single attack runs. US Navy and US Marines Corps pilots assigned flak suppression missions were exempted. US Marine Corps pilots adopted suppression tactics towards the end of 1951, using spotter aircraft that identified flak positions and then summoned fighters from CAS missions to attack them. This process evolved into a routine where US Marine Corps fighters blasted known AAA sites with gunfire, rockets, and other ordnance 30 seconds before strikers arrived. Losses were appreciably reduced.

CVG-5 used F9Fs and F2H Banshees in joint flak suppression sorties during its second combat cruise, embarked in *Essex*, in 1951–52, arming six jets with four or six 100lb VT bombs. F9F-2-equipped VF-191 of CVG-19, embarked in *Princeton*, flew many successful suppression sorties in the summer of 1952, the carrier air group reporting, "The use of jet aircraft for flak suppression was substantially increased during this period of combat, and the overall effectiveness of flak suppression [was] materially

A section of shrieking VF-831 F9F-2s (both marked with mission tallies) prepares to move towards *Antietam*'s catapults in early 1952 accompanied by the background din of massed AD Skyraiders and F4U Corsairs. A Panther was lined up with its nosewheel rolling over the catapult shuttle. An expendable bridle was attached to hooks beneath the fuselage and a hold-back arm and ring were fitted under the rear fuselage. On a signal from the catapult crew, the catapult was activated, the hold back ring fractured, and the aircraft was accelerated to 133mph in seconds. (US Navy)

increased by the use of up-to-date flak studies and target photographs in briefings. In cases where anti-aircraft gun positions were difficult to pinpoint due to terrain or camouflage, the wide area coverage of the VT-fuzed 260lb fragmentation bomb afforded sufficient blast protection to provide effective suppression. However, where the individual AA positions were prominent and easily detected, 6.5in. anti-tank rockets and 5in. HVAR proved best, both in actual damage to the positions and in the adverse psychological effect they had on enemy troops."

CVG-102's Panthers flew 1,702 sorties from *Valley Forge* between October 28, 1952 and April 22, 1953, of which 309 were for flak suppression. In January 1953, the carrier air group (which was re-designated CVG-12 the following month) published the following recommendations on tactics for effective coordinated flak suppression:

a) Conduct a joint briefing of the propeller and jet pilots. Review all known flak positions within a ten-mile radius of the target. The strike leader presents his attack plan.

b) Jets effect a running rendezvous with the earlier launched propeller strike group before reaching the target.

c) A jet flight precedes each element of the propeller group in its attacks. Repeated jet attacks afford protection for the retirement of the flight, as well as flak suppression for the following element. If it is not feasible for the jets to attack between propeller attacks the jets should make repeated runs, avoiding interference with the propeller aircrafts' attacks. Those jets not actually in an attack watch closely to pinpoint firing anti-aircraft positions.

d) Repeated firing runs into a flak area are most effective. If the jet pilot does not see the actual gun installation it is vitally important that he exert maximum fire on the coordinate fix of the reported area.

With the USAF, flak suppression was assigned to the F-80C Shooting Star – a straight-winged contemporary of the F9F. A typical mission for the aircraft was flown on May 9, 1951, when a series of NKPAF airfields were targeted. The USAF usually allocated far larger numbers of aircraft to such strikes, and on this occasion, no fewer than 312 fighters attacked the bases around Sinuiju. Forty-eight F-80s were assigned to flak suppression, each armed with two 1,000lb bombs.

The Sinuiju airfields were notorious for having some of the heaviest concentrations of 85mm and 37mm AAA to protect the MiGs and their Chinese and Soviet pilots on the ground in the nearby Antung area. Tactics employed by USAF pilots to negate the threat included pull-out from bomb delivery at 6,000ft – above the effective range of the 37mm guns.

In April and May of that year the Fifth Air Force (the FEAF's main command in-theater) lost 59 aircraft to ground fire. Test missions flown against US Army AAA

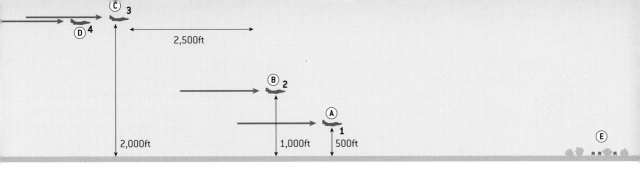

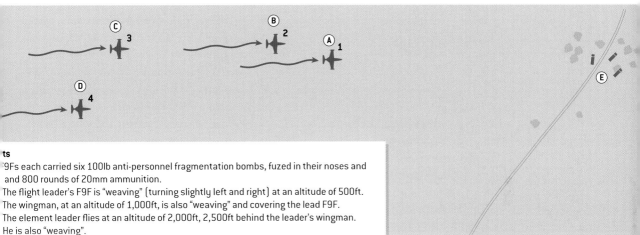

ts

9Fs each carried six 100lb anti-personnel fragmentation bombs, fuzed in their noses and and 800 rounds of 20mm ammunition.

The flight leader's F9F is "weaving" (turning slightly left and right) at an altitude of 500ft.

The wingman, at an altitude of 1,000ft, is also "weaving" and covering the lead F9F.

The element leader flies at an altitude of 2,000ft, 2,500ft behind the leader's wingman. He is also "weaving".

The element leader's wingman is at 2,000ft, in position to divert quickly to attack AAA sites.

Transportation targets are seeking cover before being attacked by F9Fs 3 and 4.

batteries revealed that – unsurprisingly – the No. 4 man in a flight of four fighters was the most vulnerable to AAA. In an attempt to reduce these losses, USAF fighter-bomber formations tended to use part of their ordnance for ad hoc flak suppression when undertaking railway attacks. Although this often had the effect of sending the gunners running for cover, it failed to destroy their weapons.

When USAF wings flew joint strikes with US Navy and US Marine Corps units, such as the July 11, 1952 assault (Operation *Pressure Pump*) on Pyongyang, which boasted one of the worst flak traps in Korea, carrier-based F9Fs supplied dedicated flak suppression divisions. There were 48 heavy guns and 100 automatic weapons defending the target area, and the strike force encountered flak at 18,000ft en route over Yongdok. Over the target, the AAA was some of the heaviest yet experienced by TF 77, reminiscent to some of World War II, and much of it was clearly radar-controlled. Effective flak suppression by diving Panthers took out five guns and silenced two more, which limited losses in 1,254 sorties to two Skyraiders.

A similar operation on August 29, 1952 launched three strikes, including aircraft from *Essex* and *Boxer*, against 40 military targets in Pyongyang. One flight in each attack group was used for flak suppression, hitting all known AAA positions that had been plotted in advance. Within days of the attack, the city's AAA defenses were doubled. Similar tactics were used for raids on metal production facilities at Sindok and Milchu, with flak-suppression Panthers leading the attacks, and re-attacking at the end of the strikes.

A single formation comprising a pair of two-aircraft sections typically used this approach profile when attacking road transportation and rail targets.

A VF-51 pilot checks the fuzes of the two 250lb bombs and a single 100lb weapon attached to the underside of his F9F-2's port wing on the flightdeck of *Essex* in early 1952. Although 500lb bombs had to be loaded with the wings spread, using a lot of space on crowded flightdecks, lighter weapons such as these could be secured to the Panther's six underwing pylons with the wings folded. Removing Mk 51 racks (for 1,000lb bombs) and Aero 14A/B rocket launchers from an F9F-5 increased its maximum speed by 40mph. (US Navy)

Large-scale attacks continued throughout the summer of 1952. On August 20, the Namyang-yi supply area on the west coast was hit by 105 aircraft from *Essex* and *Princeton*, with the US Navy strike packages being protected by an F-86 top cover. Cdr J. G. Daniels, CAG of ATG-2 embarked in *Essex*, was leading the Panther flak suppressors, and he reported that "The Air Force had given us the intelligence on the location and number of enemy AA guns, and their information was excellent. On an attack such as this, its success depends on accurate knowledge about the guns. If their exact locations are known the flak suppression aircraft can really do a job on them. Otherwise, if you are not sure of their whereabouts all you can do is strafe the general area, and that's not too effective".

Leaving the target, they were intercepted by some MiGs that penetrated the Sabre screen, but the communist pilots fired wildly and broke off when the Panthers turned to engage them.

Concentrating the defenses around high-priority targets in North Korea – more than half of the AAA guns were sited along the Yalu River between Antung and Manpoijin – was logical, but it left many areas thinly protected. In September 1952, TF 77 aircraft from *Essex*, *Princeton*, and *Boxer* hit targets on the northern borders of Korea with 259 sorties; the largest all-US Navy attack of the war. The important synthetic oil refinery at Aoji only eight miles from the Soviet border was virtually destroyed on September 1, with the attackers meeting no opposition. Clearly, the KPA had decided, unwisely, that the refinery's location made it immune from attack.

Another mission from USS *Bon Homme Richard* (CV-31) and *Princeton* on September 13, 1952 hit barracks and warehouses in Hoeryong, which was very close to the Soviet border, but only sporadic small arms fire was encountered. The B-29 force made its last major daylight strike on October 8, hitting the Kowon rail center with US Navy fighter escort. The target was known to be defended by one of the deadliest AAA traps in Korea, and on this occasion B-29s acted as flak suppressors, dropping 500lb delayed-action bombs from 21,000ft, ahead of a low-altitude US Navy strike.

AERIAL OPPOSITION

The Panther was initially seen as an air defense fighter in Korea, and its pilots had some successes against MiG-15s during CAP or escort missions, but the MiG's unexpectedly superior performance made USAF F-86 Sabres the only UN interceptors capable of matching them in aerial combat. US Navy pilots scheduled for bomber escort were starkly informed in a Navy Jet Tactics notice that "The MiG-15 [has] superior performance characteristics over the F9F and F2H." This duly meant that Panthers were primarily tasked with undertaking air-to-ground missions.

On the occasions when F9Fs were confronted by MiGs, their maneuverability and 20mm guns made them capable air-to-air fighters, despite the MiGs being 100mph faster and superior in a vertical fight. In all, nine communist aircraft (seven of which were MiG-15s) were shot down by Panther pilots for the loss of two F9Fs in aerial engagements.

On November 9, 1950, CVG-11 attacked bridges over the Yalu at Sinuiju to try and halt the flow of Chinese troops. They struck close to the main MiG-15 air base at Antung, only six miles north of the river, where the Soviet 139th Guards Fighter Aviation Regiment was based. US pilots could easily see the MiGs taking off to intercept their strike groups. To avoid entering Manchurian air space, they were also required to attack bridges side-on rather than at an angle or along the length of the structure. Pilots were forbidden to engage enemy fighters on the Manchurian side, although MiGs from Antung would cross into North Korea to attack UN aircraft operating around Sinuiju, near the Antung MiG base.

Lt Royce Williams of VF-781 points to the hole left by a 37mm cannon shell fired from a Soviet MiG-15 that hit his Panther's engine accessory section on November 18, 1952, the round knocking out the fighter's hydraulics and severing the rudder cables. With his elevators being his only effective means of control and his opponent still on his tail, Williams, who had downed four MiGs minutes earlier, dived into cloud at a lower altitude and then nursed his crippled jet (BuNo 125459) back to *Oriskany*. After removing everything of value from the F9F-5, the deck crew heaved the broken carcass – which had been holed 263 times – overboard and it disappeared into the dark sea. (US Navy)

On the 9th, VF-111 CO Lt Cdr William T. "Tom" Amen led 12 F9F-2Bs in three groups to tackle any MiGs and cover the AD Skyraider divisions. Flying over a heavily defended area, the attack aircraft were surrounded by bursting 37mm AAA shells as they dived on the bridges. As the Skyraiders pulled off their targets, having dropped their ordnance, the lead AD, flown by Lt Cdr E. T. Deacon, was quickly joined by a MiG-15 that began to fire at it.

Amen, leading his Panthers at 4,000ft, then spotted a second MiG, flown by Capt Mikhail Grachyov, closing behind him. He and wingman Ens George Holloman turned to meet the threat, closely followed by the other section (Lt(jg) Carl Dalland and Ens Earl Reimers). It was only then that MiG pilots Maj Aleksandr Stulov and Snr Lt Kaznacheev realized they were not facing USAF F-80s as they had first thought.

Capt Grachyov climbed steeply to 15,000ft and Amen stayed with him in his opponent's blind spot, shooting when he could, as did the remaining three F9F pilots. Eventually, Grachyov decided to dive, and Amen went with him, accelerating past 500mph and then having to extend his dive brakes as his Panther, borrowed from fellow CVG-11 F9F-2B squadron VF-112, reached its Mach limits. The MiG continued in a steepening dive through 3,000ft and rolled inverted, but the jets were heading for mountainous terrain. Amen concluded that the MiG pilot was "either nuts, or he had a wonderful airplane." Although he just managed to pull up with 200ft clearance, the MiG impacted the mountain side and exploded. The Sinuiju bridge was damaged and needed to be re-attacked. Perhaps more significantly, the US Navy had scored the first MiG-15 shoot-down, with Capt Mikhail Grachyov becoming the first Soviet pilot to be killed in combat during the Korean War.

November 18, 1952 also proved to be an unlucky date for MiG pilots. *Oriskany*'s air group, CVG-102, included VF-781 and VF-783 (later re-designated VF-121 and

VF-831's F9F-2 BuNo 127149 suffered serious AAA damage during the squadron's first combat cruise embarked in *Antietam* in 1951–52. It was quickly repaired and sent back into action. The communist deployment of modern AAA in defense of key transport routes during the autumn of 1951 greatly increased the potential for such damage to be inflicted on Panthers during low-level attacks. Indeed, in October 1951 alone, ten F9Fs limped back to *Antietam* after they had sustained heavy battle damage, although they were repaired and returned to service. Most had suffered damaged wings and vertical stabilizers (as seen here), although in one case the aircraft had sustained a holed nose and shattered windscreen. (US Navy)

VF-122, respectively), which were giving the F9F-5 its combat debut. That day, TF 77's carriers were sailing off Chongjin, not far from Soviet bases at Vladivostok, and air strikes were to be flown against factory buildings at Hoeryong, on the Yalu River, which was well within range of Soviet fighters. Seeing the need for an F9F-5 CAP, TF 77 instructed CVG-102 to have Panthers patrol between its vessels and Vladivostok as a precaution.

Distances were crucial, as a Panther CAP needed a jet intruder such as an Ilyushin Il-28 bomber to be detected within 150 miles of the carrier in order to attempt an interception in time. Lt Claire Elwood's division from VF-781 launched into a blizzard to intercept "bogies" heading for the carrier. Section leader Lt Royce Williams sighted the contrails of seven MiG-15s far above at 40,000ft. Shortly thereafter, Elwood and wingman Lt(jg) John Middleton withdrew to lower altitude with a fuel pump failure. As Williams and his wingman Lt(jg) David Rowlands reached 26,000ft, the silver MiGs dived on them in two groups, intending to box them in.

Williams turned behind the No. 4 jet and fired. It fell away, smoking. CVG-102's After Action Report recorded that Rowlands, although having fired all of his ammunition at the aircraft, "followed the crippled MiG down to 8,000ft where it was last seen smoking in a steep, graveyard spiral. Gun camera film confirmed the kill." Williams' second victim was the flight leader's wingman, whose jet went down in flames after a long burst of 20mm fire. He was then left to fight three MiGs, which were soon joined by the flight leader and his remaining two wingmen.

Williams repeatedly fired short bursts during the course of the wild dogfight that ensued, constantly turning towards his attackers while trying to protect his own "six o'clock" without a wingman. The MiGs, faster and more maneuverable, fired wildly from a distance and repeatedly overshot. Then the section leader was engaged and Williams saw parts flying off the aircraft as the MiG dived away with its airbrakes extended. One Soviet pilot managed to fire his cannon from behind the F9F, hitting its wing and knocking out all the hydraulics apart from the elevators. The jet followed Williams as he dived into clouds.

By now Rowlands and Middleton had entered the fray, firing on another MiG until its pilot ejected. Rowlands then drove away Williams' pursuer as the latter emerged from cloud at 400ft, too low to eject and heading for the carrier while dodging AAA from US Navy destroyers that mis-identified him. His jet was uncontrollable below 195mph, so he had to trap back aboard *Oriskany* at that speed. The Panther had 263 holes from 23mm and 37mm hits, and its battered remains were pushed overboard.

Although Williams was only credited with one MiG victory and a "probable" following the eight-minute fight, US radar intelligence together with subsequent Russian revelations indicated that three Soviet MiGs were shot down and the fourth crash-landed, killing the pilot, flight leader Capt Nikolai Belyakov. His wingman, Snr Lt Aleksandr Vandaev, was also killed, and Snr Lt Vladimir Pakhomkin's MiG-15 lost so much fuel following combat damage that it eventually crashed into the sea along with its pilot. Political sensitivities about the long-term effects of a direct conflict with Soviet-based aircraft meant that Williams' achievement was suppressed. The November 18 fight was at least a reminder that the Naval Aviators flying Panthers were primarily fighter pilots.

Thanks to their aircraft's unmatched ability to climb to high altitudes, MiG pilots routinely chose not to engage F9Fs in the skies over North Korea. This was indeed the case on May 9, 1951, when Sinuiju airfield, with recently installed heavy AAA defenses, was the target for a large Fifth Air Force attack. On this occasion, CAP was provided by US Marine Corps F9Fs and F-84 Thunderjets from the 27th Fighter Wing. Although around 50 MiGs took off from Antung in response to the raid, their pilots showed a marked reluctance to engage the American fighters, allowing the attackers to destroy all aircraft on the base and much of its air-to-ground defense capability.

Joint operations with USAF bombers subsequently became routine following this mission. The first to involve US Navy jets occurred on August 25, 1951, when 11 F9F-2s from VF-51 and 12 F2H-2s from VF-172 sortied from *Essex* as escorts for 35 B-29s attacking Rashin marshaling yard, less than 25 miles from the Soviet border and beyond the range of USAF Sabres in South Korea – but well within range of Soviet and Chinese MiG-15s. The Panthers stayed close to the B-29s, while the Banshees, with better high-altitude performance, flew top cover. No MiGs appeared and AAA was insignificant. The following day, VF-51 flew an interdiction mission over Majon-ni, and as Lt(jg) Moore reported, there was "lots of anti-aircraft fire. We all got hit and didn't see a damn thing."

A massive, coordinated attack on North Korea's hydroelectric power network began on June 23, 1952. It supplied power to industries and cities both in North Korea and China. US Navy jets entered "MiG Alley" for the first time since the November 9, 1950 Yalu bridges attack. Aircraft (including 18 F9Fs) from four carriers were sent against the primary Sui-ho generating plant (the world's fourth largest), two plants at Fusen and four at Kyusen, while USAF bombers struck Sui-ho and six other generating sites. There were 44 heavy AAA guns and 37 automatic weapons, manned by the best crews and known to be unusually accurate, defending Sui-ho and its subsidiary plants.

That same day, Choshin No. 3 generating station was hit by 38 F9Fs from Marine Air Group 33. Flak suppression was delegated to Fifth Air Force F-84s and F-51Ds while the US Marine Corps Panthers and Corsairs carried out the strike.

Thirty-five Panthers from Lt Cdr William Jernigan's VF-24, embarked in *Boxer*, Cdr John Sweeney's VF-112, from *Princeton*, and Cdr James Rowney's VF-191, on board *Philippine Sea*, effectively strafed some very active flak

Lt(jg) Richard Clinite, a VF-153 pilot on his second combat tour, shows off the damage to his F9F-5 caused by large-caliber AAA during an attack on a major target in early May 1953. This aircraft was later repaired on board *Princeton* with sections from another F9F-5. A few days after this incident, on May 13, Clinite was hit again by AAA while flying another Panther, forcing him to eject over Wonsan harbor. A rescue helicopter was quickly on the scene, but strong gusts of wind whipped up the surface of the water and prevented Clinite from collapsing his parachute, and he drowned before he could be recovered. (US Navy)

sites at Sui-ho, dropping 250lb bombs while Skyraiders hit the plant. The ADs were followed in by USAF fighter-bombers, and the whole operation was watched over by a MiGCAP of 84 F-86s and a TARCAP of Panthers. The subsequent After Action Report noted that "The flak suppression was terrific. The AAA really looked rough when the jets [F9Fs] first went in. After they made their runs, there was nothing to it. They really did a job."

The strike force spent only two minutes over the target, during which time they virtually destroyed their main powerhouse target and sustained AAA damage to only five aircraft. Pyongyang, many factories, and large residential areas were left without power. As the target was close to the Manchurian border, the strike force also experienced heavy AAA from within that sanctuary area. They saw "intense machine gun fire, continuous predicted fire from heavy weapons and automatic anti-aircraft fire," bursting accurately at various levels up to 10,000ft.

Lt Don Engen had firsthand experience of the Manchurian AAA sites. "They had a lot of heavy-caliber AAA down there that they could shoot at us from China but we couldn't shoot back. CAG Harvey Lanham [with Don as wingman] was coordinating bridge attacks, so we stayed at 35,000ft. I was hearing this 'popcorn' going off, so I knew they were getting kind of close. The sky was black behind us. We were the two guys orbiting up there, and these guys were practicing with their guns and it was really thick, but we vectored people onto the bridges and they were successful. Harvey and I then dropped down to strafe, and I recall flying down the Yalu River at 100ft. I figured if the Chinese are going to shoot at me they're going to hit North Koreans [and vice versa], but this didn't bother them at all. They just continued shooting."

The US Navy squadrons successfully attacked more hydroelectric power network targets over two days in August 1952, losing only two aircraft to ground fire in 546 sorties. The operation was the first time that US Navy and US Marine Corps aircraft had joined USAF units in attacking the same targets, and it resulted in the destruction of more than 90 percent of North Korea's electricity generation capacity.

F9F-5s had replaced F4U Corsairs on most carriers by 1953, and their losses consequently mounted as TF 77 flew increasing numbers of dangerous armed reconnaissance missions. On VF-111's October 1951 to July 1952 cruise embarked in *Valley Forge*, F9F-2s and F9F-2Ps flew 51 per cent of the missions – 3,667 against 1,525 by Corsairs. Between July 1952 and July 1953, 44 F9Fs were lost as the volume of ground fire steadily increased and more radar-guided AAA batteries appeared in-theater.

Despite the heightened threat of being shot down, Panthers undertaking low-altitude attacks on targets of opportunity still frequently yielded spectacular results. A January 16, 1953 armed reconnaissance sortie by VF-51 F9F-5s (which were hit 26 times during the unit's third cruise, embarked in *Valley Forge*, in 1952–53, ten times by heavy- and medium-caliber guns and 16 times by small arms) discovered an active railway complex near Wonsan and strafed the trains with 20mm fire. Follow-up attacks by F4U-4s from VF-92 and AD-4s from VF-54, both also flying from *Valley Forge*, destroyed or seriously damaged 60 railcars.

CVG-12's VF-781 and VF-783, embarked in *Oriskany*, were also heavily engaged in armed reconnaissance missions throughout this period, with F9F pilots averaging 66 sorties each during the October 1952 to April 1953 cruise.

OPPOSITE

On August 29, 1952, US Navy and US Marine Corps F9Fs attacked a locomotive repair depot and other buildings in Pyongyang, inflicting major damage. Targeting North Korea's well-developed rail network comprised a major share of the UN air attacks throughout the war. Amongst the anti-aircraft defenses that ringed the repair depot were several ZPU-4 four-barreled 14.5mm heavy machine guns, depicted here engaging the departing Panthers seconds after they had released their ordnance. The ZPU-4 was the most complex of the ZPU series weapons, originally using M1910 "Russian Maxim" guns in single, double, or triple mounts.

"CHEROKEE"

In October 1952 communist forces were obviously massing troops for another ground offensive in the new year, so, lacking any strategic targets, carrier air groups concentrated on troop and supply targets near the frontline beyond artillery range. A photographic survey of the area revealed numerous supply concentrations, tunnels, and truck parks.

A typical "Cherokee" strike included eight F4U-4s, eight AD-4s, and up to 12 Panthers on "general support" (rather than interdiction) missions, the latter being planned to cause maximum damage within a short time so that attacking aircraft were not exposed to excessive levels of AAA fire. Unlike CAS missions, "Cherokee" strikes had dedicated flak suppression flights whose aircraft were armed with anti-personnel bombs. This meant that strike aircraft did not have to use their ordnance knocking out unforeseen AAA sites. Furthermore, strike aircraft were not required to remain over the target for extended periods, as they were when providing CAS.

For the first "Cherokee" on October 9, VF-821 provided eight F9Fs led by unit CO Cdr D. W. Cooper for flak suppression – and there was plenty of opposition. A VA-702 Skyraider pilot reported that "Much enemy flak was encountered on these missions, and pilots usually considered a 'Cherokee' strike as 'hot'." The Kumwha sector, known as "Artillery Valley," was a particularly "hot" area, but a rain of 2,000lb bombs quickly reduced the Chinese AAA threat.

"Cherokees" were described by the US Eighth Army as "air power's most potent contribution to the Korean War in its present static-front condition." By mid-October more than half of TF 77's strikes were "Cherokees." From March 1953 until war's end, the F9Fs' flak suppression efforts were often combined with US Army long-range artillery fire.

CVG-12 pilots noticed a steady increase in AAA, reporting that "it has become more difficult to suppress effectively." If re-attacks were needed on consecutive days, pilots were given enlarged photographs of known enemy AAA positions in the target area. They found them "exceedingly helpful in locating an exact position by physical appearance, rather than just a general position marked on a map."

In the final three months of the war Panther squadrons were increasingly active. *Boxer*'s ATG-1 had three F9F units – VF-52 and VF-151 with F9F-2s and VF-111 (later exchanged for an F4U unit) with F9F-5s. They were in constant demand, with May 19, 1953, when 107 sorties were launched, being a typical day during the deployment. The cruise report noted, "In the vicinity of Pukchong, F9Fs destroyed 52 buildings and damaged others. In the afternoon, Panthers made 27 hits in destroying ten buildings and bunkers on the coast northeast of Songjin."

On May 24 the cruise report stated that "Two F9F strikes between Songjin and Hungnam resulted in 12 rail cuts and damage to a train, trucks, and troop concentrations. CAS missions by F9Fs on the eastern front resulted in five road cuts and damage to three automatic weapons." VF-52 even took on night "heckler" missions in May, using the F9F-2's quiet approach to pounce on road traffic. Four Panthers, led by unit CO Lt Cdr James Kinsella, caught a convoy by surprise and destroyed nine trucks, badly damaging 14 others. Gunners were unable to track the fast-moving jets.

An all-US Navy series of strikes to assist RoK troops in recapturing Anchor Hill on June 15 was described as "the heaviest naval air blow of the conflict" by CVG-9, embarked in *Philippine Sea*. It required an unprecedented 703 sorties by aircraft from

Princeton (CVG-15) and *Philippine Sea*, and cost communist forces 3,000 casualties. In some of the final sorties of the war, Panthers from both carriers hit airfields at Yonpo, Koeman, and Hamhung West on July 27 while the ceasefire agreement with North Korea was being signed.

US MARINE CORPS

VMF-311, the first US Marine Corps unit to fly jets in combat, was based at the former NKPAF airfield at K-27 Yonpo with the 1st MAW from December 7, 1950. The squadron commenced operations three days later when Panthers provided CAS for Marines fighting for their survival near the Choisin Reservoir. Unit CO Lt Col Neil MacIntyre and Maj Earl Crowe flew the first mission, and they were "greeted" by flak, MacIntyre described how "On one run I had reached my pull-out and was watching Earl's run when I noticed something strange. His tracers weren't quite right. I called, 'Earl, did you fire on that last run?' Pretty soon Earl comes back 'No'. The light dawns – the tracers were going the wrong way. 'Earl, I guess someone's shooting at us then'."

VMF-311 had to evacuate to K-9 Pusan on December 13, along with most of the Marine Air units in-theater, when Chinese forces surged south and occupied Yonpo. The primitive muddy conditions synonymous with Korean airfields rapidly wore the Panthers down, and by January 25, 1951 they were in such bad shape that the unit was transferred to Itami, in Japan, for overhaul. VMF-311 had lost three F9Fs by then, two of them in combat.

Tactics to reduce exposure to AAA after 11 aircraft were damaged in June 1951 included a minimum 1,000ft altitude for armed reconnaissance and a sustained speed of 345mph over the target. On one mission 16 Panthers made a concerted attack on AAA sites in a heavily defended town, dropping all their bombs in a single pass. Several gun positions were destroyed before they could respond to the surprise attack.

VMF-311's reputation for aggressive flying was underlined by numerous confrontations with MiGs which resulted in one loss. An F9F-2B flown by 1Lt Robert Bell was hit when four Panthers strayed into Manchuria on July 21, 1951 to cover the attempted recovery of a shot-down MiG. His division was attacked by 15 MiG-15s and Bell was shot down. He spent the rest of the war as a PoW.

VMF-311 was joined at Pohang by F9F-4-equipped VMF-115 on February 15, 1952. On an early rail-cut mission, the jet of unit CO Lt Col Thomas Coles was hit by an 85mm shell that blew off its nosecone and wrecked the gun installation. As Lt Col Coles described it, "One moment I was traveling in excess of 500mph and the next I was doing 180mph as if I had hit a brick wall." He had to "outrun the mass of tracers and big, black and horrible fiery red exploding fireworks" to reach an emergency landing strip.

An unnamed pilot from VMF-311 mops his brow for the benefit of the photographer after he had a lucky escape when the starboard wingtip tank of his F9F-2 exploded following a hit by AAA. The pilot managed to land his jet at K-3 Pohang without any further dramas. (US Marine Corps)

Lt Col Darrell Irwin, CO of VMF-311, stands up in the cockpit of his F9F-2B (BuNo 123451) after returning to K-3 Pohang at the end of yet another successful mission in May 1952. Irwin commanded the squadron from late February through to early June 1952. Note the large number of mission symbols painted on the fuselage of his aircraft. This jet was credited with flying 445 missions (totaling 1,002 combat hours) during its time with the 1st MAW. (US Marine Corps)

After various engine compressor problems, VMF-115's F9F-4s were exchanged for more reliable F9F-2s in April.

Sometimes, automatic weapons caused unseen damage. The F9F-2 of VMF-311's Capt John Bostwick rolled over and crashed near enemy troops during an attack on supply dumps and artillery on May 10, 1951. Although no ground fire was seen, several machine guns opened up on his division as they circled the site of the crash. On January 3, 1952, squadronmate Maj George N. Major reported hits during an armed reconnaissance mission at 2,000ft, but he thought the damage was not serious. Minutes later, his jet suddenly dived straight into the ground.

Marine Air regarded CAS as its primary function, using tactics developed during World War II. Flak suppression was vital for each mission. A leading section usually took that responsibility, preparing the way for the other two Panthers to bomb a target. In 1951, Marine pilots found flak either non-existent or surprisingly heavy, and it was often hard to predict which would apply despite daily updates to VMF-311's Flak Situation Map. The many AAA sites around bridges were frequent targets. Some had up to five guns in them. However, as Robert Futrell's official history of the USAF war effort in Korea stated, "The flak suppression strikes usually drove enemy gunners under cover, but seldom destroyed enemy weapons."

Enemy flak was not the only danger facing Panther pilots. On June 14, 1952, incorrectly set VT fuzes resulted in two losses for VMF-115 when Capt Howard Campbell's F9F-2 exploded shortly after take-off. The premature detonation of his 260lb fragmentation bombs also fatally damaged his wingman's Panther. Ten other pilots had to jettison their "frag" bombs when they armed themselves too early during the same mission, officially due to improper installation of arming wires.

On another mission, Maj Henry Hise, leading VMF-311 Panthers armed with similar VT bombs, called his flight. "I told them if the propeller on their bomb fuzes starts to spin, jettison them immediately. We made an approach [to Pyongyang] above broken clouds and encountered some radar-directed heavy AAA breaking just below the formation. I broke up the flight and got rid of the bombs on the airfield. It was a great relief."

US Marine Corps Panthers took part in some of the most decisive single missions of the war, including the devastating October 4, 1952 raid on the KPA tank and infantry school that also involved no fewer than 285 USAF aircraft. During the final months of the war, both VMF-115 and VMF-311 used the ground-based MPQ radar bombing system for some missions, dropping ordnance in poor weather on a signal from a radar tracker. The two squadrons were still in action on the final day of fighting in Korea, flying CAS for US Marine Corps outposts on the frontline. Capt Will Armagost of VMF-311 undertook the final Marine Air mission 35 minutes before the ceasefire, destroying a supply dump with four 500lb bombs.

PHOTO-RECCE PANTHERS

TF 77 generated most of its own reconnaissance data, processing imagery aboard the carriers. VC-61 had three-aircraft detachments of camera-equipped F9F-2Ps (and F9F-5Ps from November 1952) with carrier air groups in-theater from November 1950, these jets surveying important bridges and airfields at four-day intervals, providing bomb damage assessment and weekly photo intelligence. The detachments also photo-mapped the rail network in eastern Korea during 1951 so that AAA installations could be avoided. Early the following year, CVG-11's VC-61 Det C, flying from *Philippine Sea*, modified its F9F-2Ps fitted with F-56 20in. cameras to shoot aerial oblique color transparencies.

Among the 100+ daily sorties usually launched from a carrier in fair weather were several "jet reccos" by the VC-61 detachment. Lt(jg) John Moore escorted an F9F-2P on one such mission on August 23, 1951. "To get his pictures, the recco pilot had to set himself a course at 500ft and fly absolutely straight despite AA fire. He was kind of a sitting duck. We would make a run up the valley and turn around on another run, and all the time they were shooting at him." Moore blasted one of the hilltop AAA sites, recalling "It was like swatting flies."

One of the more successful missions by a VC-61 F9F-2P brought back detailed photos of the small town of Kapsan in the northeastern mountains, where covert intelligence sources had reported that a meeting of top PVA and KPA generals and senior politicians was to take place. The VC-61 pictures of the compound enabled a strike force, including four VF-831 Panthers, to eliminate the target, killing no fewer than 509 personnel and destroying the entire records of the North Korean Communist Party. F9F flak suppressors led the attack, followed by VT bomb-carrying F4Us to eliminate AAA positions, which had fired intensely. It was one of the few missions where TF 77 aviators felt that they had achieved a significant, lasting success.

With photo-reconnaissance Panther missions usually being flown at low altitudes and maximum speed, the "photo-bird" and its F9F escort always struggled with fuel shortages. Indeed, VF-111's F9F-5 BuNo 126204 "ran dry" while escorting an F2H-2P during a photo-reconnaissance mission from *Boxer* on June 19, 1953, forcing Lt D. H. Opsahl to ditch. As CVG-4 (embarked in *Lake Champlain*) reported in 1953, "The F9F is short-legged when compared to the F2H Banshee [the carrier air group's VC-62 Det 44 was equipped with F2H-2Ps]. The margin of time is very slim when working a 90-minute schedule."

Four F9F-2Ps were lost on operations during the Korean War, but only one of these aircraft (from VC-61 Det D of CVG-15, embarked in USS *Antietam* (CV-36)) was written off as a direct result of flak damage.

F9F-2Ps had a single camera window, while F9F-5Ps had windows on both sides. F2H-2P Banshees supplemented the photo-Panthers from 1951, their two USAF K-38 36in. cameras "enabling them to photograph high intensity flak areas at 1,500ft and still obtain scales suitable for flak analysis." Only one target run was needed, whereas a K-17-equipped F9F-2P needed three passes. This VC-61 Det C F9F-2P is preparing to launch from *Philippine Sea* in 1952. (US Navy)

STATISTICS AND ANALYSIS

When China entered the Korean War, the KPA's AAA defenses rapidly expanded. By May 1951, the official UN estimate of heavy guns, mainly 85mm M1939s, had already risen to 275, with 600 automatic weapons. Near the end of the war, an estimated 786 heavy guns, mainly 85mm M1939s and 76mm M1938s were also in-theater with four Soviet AAA divisions. No fewer than 1,672 automatic weapons were available too, some being issued to volunteer "Hunter Groups" who received rewards if they downed three UN aircraft within 90 days. The M1939s were sited mainly around the main railway marshaling yards and vital bridges in batteries of two to eight guns.

In 1950, few 85mm batteries had radar guidance, which meant accuracy was generally poor. By late 1952 almost all had radar units, forcing B-29s to bomb from altitudes in excess of 20,000ft, with consequently reduced accuracy. UN reconnaissance and intelligence reports showed that by March 1953 there were 32 sets of gun-laying radars controlling 222 guns, and 37 batteries with eight heavy guns, half of them radar-controlled.

With the increased AAA, fighter-bombers were also forced to attack from altitudes that degraded accurate weapons delivery. Heavily defended sites forced mission planners to decide whether re-attacking targets which had been destroyed and rebuilt several times was feasible, given the likely aircraft losses. Many resulted from North Korean barrage firing or releasing concentrations of gunfire ("a sheet of bullets" as Royal Navy Sea Fury pilot Lt Harry Hands put it) into the paths of attacking aircraft. US Navy losses to AAA remained high between July 1951 and the end of hostilities. Of the 384 US Navy aircraft lost to flak from that point on in the conflict, 57 of them were F9Fs. The lion's share were F4Us, with 193 being shot down.

Supply routes were usually defended by 37mm automatic weapons – a major threat to low-flying F9F interdiction flights. Around two-thirds of North Korea's automatic weapons were used to counter interdiction operations. Larger numbers of small arms and machine guns engaging most targets at low altitudes posed more of a threat to F9Fs than heavy AAA weapons. Of 73 cases of loss or damage to CVG-5 aircraft in 1951, only nine were attributable to heavier guns. A USAF report in August 1952 estimated that 79 percent of losses were due to automatic weapons. Small arms were responsible for seven percent and heavy guns for 14 percent. Lighter weapons were also responsible for 97 percent of the damage to aircraft that returned to base with hits.

Many of the casualties suffered by the Fifth Air Force and TF 77 were out of production, irreplaceable World War II-era aircraft such as F4U-4s and F-51Ds. Although new jets appeared, there was a net reduction in the overall numbers of interdiction aircraft. In addition to outright losses, there was consistent severe, costly damage inflicted on hundreds of aircraft, grounding them for long periods. Although F9Fs could use their speed to evade flak, slower piston-engined types were better for tackling AAA positions in valleys and mountainous terrain. Jets also survived AAA damage better than the F4U, which flew many flak-suppression sorties. The Corsair's oil cooler was particularly vulnerable to damage because its bypass mechanism had been removed in an effort to save costs. This meant that just one bullet hole could rapidly drain the oil out of the engine.

Communist forces concentrated AAA defenses around the relatively few high-priority targets in North Korea. Combining weapons of several calibers in one area gave the gunners flexibility in tackling targets at different speeds and altitudes. Major centers and target areas such as Pyongyang, Sinuiju, and the Sui-ho hydroelectric

Maj Gen Frank Lowe, who was President Harry S. Truman's representative in Korea during the early months of the conflict, examines captured KPA AAA in Pyongyang on October 21, 1950. The weaponry was found near the monument commemorating the liberation of North Korea by the Soviet Union in 1945. Gen Paek Sun Yup, leading the 1st RoK division into the city, observed that North Korean soldiers were "throwing away their weapons as we met them." The PVA retook the city on December 5 and the US Eighth Army retreated south, having suffered 11,000 casualties. (Truman Library 66-4466)

F9F-5 BuNo 126204 from VF-111 flies over Korea in the spring of 1953. On June 19, while escorting an F2H-2P during a photo-reconnaissance mission from *Boxer*, this Panther ran out of fuel and its pilot, Lt D. H. Opsahl, had to ditch it off the Korean coast. He was rescued by helicopter, having sustained back injuries when the jet hit the water. VF-111 crossdecked to *Lake Champlain* just days later, and the embarked CVG-4 was quick to label the F9F-5 "short-legged" on range compared with the F2H-2s flown by the carrier air group's VF-22 and VF-62. (US Navy)

dam were protected by more than 59 percent of the heavy AAA weaponry in North Korea by September 1952.

Railway lines and main supply routes were defended by 46 percent of the KPA's automatic anti-aircraft guns, principally 37mm weapons, but they also had 31 percent of the 76mm and 85mm guns. Many F9Fs were lost attacking the communist rail network, and as Maj Frank Merrill wrote in his US Army Command and General Staff College paper *A Study of Aerial Interdiction of Railways During the Korean War* in 1965, "The ability of the Chinese and North Koreans to keep their rail lines operative in the face of constant air attacks was nothing short of phenomenal."

NKPAF airfields were so frequently attacked that attempts to defend them were largely abandoned by mid-1952. Bases such as Namsi and Taechon were ringed by numerous automatic weapons, but their radars proved ineffective against fast, maneuvering jets. These defenses were removed as the airfields became unusable, and by mid-1952 only Sinuiju and Pyongyang airfields were defended.

Mobility was a key element in the use of anti-aircraft defenses. If critical targets like bridges, forward storage areas or dams were repeatedly attacked, it was usually possible to transport towed weapons to those areas, typically at night. For the FEAF and TF 77, the lack of information on these unexpected defenses complicated mission planning.

UN planners regarded North Korea's defenses as comparatively light, at least compared with Nazi Germany's in World War II, which many USAF pilots in Korea had experienced a few years previously. Good photo intelligence and planning could enable pilots to avoid concentrations of flak. However, the constant threat of AAA was wearing, as Lt Don Engen recalled. "Fatigue and getting shot at take a toll. When you come back and somebody else is missing it begins to get to you." When pilots saw that the damage they inflicted on bridges and railways was always repaired within days, the effect on morale was corrosive.

The simple measure of the success enjoyed by the communist gunners is the number of aircraft losses that can be accurately attributed to their gunfire. In all, 816 UN aircraft were lost to ground fire, compared with 147 in aerial engagements. Set against the total of 736,439 sorties flown, the attrition rate was a low 0.17 percent. More aircraft (945) were written off in operational accidents.

Piston-engined fighters were around three times more vulnerable to AAA than jets and the F-51 suffered the most, with 95 percent of the Mustangs lost being downed by ground fire. The US Navy's F4U force also suffered high attrition, with an estimated 75 percent of the Corsair lost falling to flak. The aircraft proved far more vulnerable to ground fire than the F9F, suffering twice as many hits.

The USAF calculated that the loss rate for propeller-driven aircraft was three times that of jets. Partly, this was because reciprocating engines, in the aircraft's nose and often liquid-cooled, were more exposed to flak than jet engines, buried in the fighter's fuselage. Also, the higher speeds and lower noise levels of jets on approach obviously made them more difficult targets. Occasionally, there were uncertainties about Panthers attributed to both MiG pilots and AAA. VMF-311's F9F-2 BuNo 123593, recorded as a loss to flak on October 4, 1951, was also claimed by MiG-15 pilot Snr Lt Mikhail Zykov, who mistook it for an F-80A.

Despite their considerable defenses, occupying large numbers of troops, 18 out of North Korea's 22 main cities had been largely ruined by war's end, leaving US jets with few worthwhile targets. However, AAA positions often survived, as flak suppression would frequently damage but not destroy the heavier weapons.

North Korean and Chinese gunners exacted a heavy price on the UN interdiction campaign, but overall losses actually fell during the conflict, declining from 0.18 per sortie in 1950 to 0.07 for 1953. Total combat losses of 1,230 aircraft for all three services to ground fire averaged out to 0.17 per sortie.

Individual Soviet-operated AAA units made over-generous claims. The 64th Fighter Aviation Corps' AAA units, for example, claimed 153 UN aircraft during three years of combat, while its fighter regiments claimed 1,250 – more than the overall total of all UN combat losses. Soviet statistics also showed that an average of 560 85mm rounds, or 630 37mm rounds or up to 3,000 rounds of 12.7mm ammunition were required to shoot down each UN aircraft.

Interdiction by fighter-bombers like the F9F, relying on visual detection of targets of opportunity followed by strafing with gunfire or sustained rocket firing, necessitated low-altitude missions. The lessons of World War II, when similar attacks became extremely hazardous, had to be re-learned in Korea. From January to May 1952, the loss and severe damage rates for aircraft flying low-altitude missions rose to 21.6 aircraft per 1,000 sorties. Between March 1951 and June 1952, the numbers of aircraft hit increased from 202 (from *Boxer*) to 551 (from *Valley Forge*).

Aircraft were often struck as they pulled out from dive attacks. The US Navy duly raised the minimum pull-out altitude to 3,000ft, while the USAF calculated that half of the ground fire hits on its aircraft occurred below 2,500ft, and it also ordered a 3,000ft pull-out from August 1952. Prior to the implementation of these restrictions,

When the tailhook of VF-84 F9F-5 BuNo 125232 refused to deploy at the end of a flight from *Lake Champlain* during CVG-8's 1954– 55 Mediterranean cruise, the pilot was forced to take the barrier. Broken tailhooks also caused accidents throughout the war. One of *Valley Forge*'s F9F squadrons logged 15 deck crashes in the first three weeks of the conflict, followed by a further 20 in July 1950. During that time, AAA had inflicted just one bullet hole in a Panther. (US Navy)

US Navy and USAF pilots had been used to flying much lower, and some continued to do so in order to detect or hit their targets successfully. The altitude restriction did approximately halve losses in the second part of 1952, although this improvement was also due to choosing a wider variety of targets. When the altitude restriction was lifted in early June 1953, losses rose again – the USAF had 17 of its new F-86F Sabre fighter-bombers shot down between June 6 and July 20.

Although the F9F, in seven sub-types, flew with 23 US Navy squadrons on 23 combat deployments and served with two land-based US Marine Corps units in-theater, the twin-engined F2H Banshee and its photo-reconnaissance F2H-2P version were superior in speed, combat ceiling, and endurance. The McDonnell fighter entered service in March 1949 and subsequently equipped US Navy and US Marine Corps units, but it could not fly fighter-bomber missions until August 1951 with VF-172 when *Essex* received more powerful steam catapults.

Despite concern over the unexpected MiG-15 threat, only five US Navy and US Marine Corps aircraft were known to have fallen to the communist jet fighter. AAA was the certain, or most likely cause of most of the other losses. Fighters were the most frequent combat casualties, with 400 losses including 64 Panthers, mainly in ground attack situations.

However, the hazards of seaborne operations accounted for the largest proportion of US Navy and US Marine Corps casualties. Non-combat losses cost 740 aircraft, including 56 that suffered shrapnel damage from their own weapons or crashed when their pilots became fixated on a target. More Panthers were lost to "cold shot" catapult accidents than to AAA during the early cruises, but on CVG-5's second cruise (embarked in *Essex* from June 26, 1951 to March 25, 1952), CAG Cdr Marshall U. Beebe calculated that his carrier air group got through two sets of aircraft due to AAA battle damage and intensive use. In three months during 1951, his aircraft were hit 318 times, 27 were lost and 11 pilots were killed.

Conversely, VF-111 lost six Panthers flying with CVG-11 from *Philippine Sea* in 1950–51, but only one of these jets was downed by enemy fire.

The interdiction effort, the main thrust of UN activity in the war, cost both sides dearly, while concerted strikes on key targets like the hydroelectric network or airfields inflicted deeper wounds on the North Korean war effort. In both types of warfare the F9F, despite its limited payload, was of great importance as a flak suppressor, ground-attacker, air-to-air fighter, and reconnaissance aircraft. When strikes on the railway lines and bridges in the Chongchon area were intensified in January 1953, UN fighter-bombers flew 1,166 sorties, of which no fewer than 713 were to suppress AAA.

One US Marine Corps F9F-2 from VMF-311 completed an incredible 445 combat missions totaling 1,002 hours of flying during early 1952, with many of these missions seeing the jet bombing rail targets. In a major attack on Chongjin in April 1952 by 110 CVG-2 and -11 aircraft, only three received superficial damage. The lack of losses on this mission was attributed to the Panthers that were "sent in ahead on flak-suppression runs and effectively silenced the AAA," according to the CVG-3 After Action Report. *Princeton*'s 1953 cruise report stated emphatically that, "On all strikes the flak encountered was much less effective when jet flak suppression was present. Jet flak suppression is a 'must' against heavily defended targets if the mission is to be carried out successfully."

AFTERMATH

Soviet policy in arming North Korea included the provision of substantial quantities of AAA, although it was generally obsolete and had already been phased out of service in the USSR. The Soviet government was unwilling to risk its newest defense acquisitions in this proxy war.

The conflict revealed deficiencies in US equipment and strategies which remained unresolved when the Vietnam War commenced a decade later. A basic reason for the failure to curtail the communist transport network was highlighted by Gen Earle E. Partridge, commanding general of the Fifth Air Force, in April 1951 when he commented "I believe that the paramount deficiency of the USAF today is our inability to effectively seek out and destroy the enemy at night." The US Navy could not remedy this shortcoming until the introduction of the A-6 Intruder in 1963.

Dependence upon World War II-stock unguided iron bombs was clearly an inefficient way of attacking most targets in North Korea. Until laser-guided weapons were fielded by the USAF late in the Vietnam War, the same "sledgehammer" approach was used – the US Navy resisted the use of "smart weapons" in Vietnam. By the time US aircraft faced communist AAA over North Vietnam 12 years after the conflict in Korea had ended, the general use of proximity fuzes had increased the lethality of the heavy guns

F9F-8 Cougars of VA-192 escort an F9F-8P of VFP-61 DET E off the coast of Formosa during CVG-19's 1957 WestPac embarked in USS *Yorktown* (CVA-10). Cougars replaced Panthers in frontline units from late 1952, although no F9F-8s saw combat over Korea. (US Navy)

by around 500 percent. Even so, North Korea's AAA defenses imposed a punitive cost on the USA. As a US Navy Interim Evaluation Report for May to December 1951 put it:

> It is doubtful whether the interdiction campaign in Korea has been as costly to the enemy as to the US. The enemy has lost many vehicles, much rolling stock and supplies and has suffered heavy physical destruction of property, but it is doubtful whether this has placed a greater strain on the economies of North Korea, China, and the USSR than upon the economy of the US. The cost of maintaining interdiction forces in or near Korea, the cost of hundreds of aircraft lost and tons of munitions and supplies consumed, and the expenditure of national resources have been keenly felt. While the cost of the war assumes fantastic proportions for the US, the enemy largely offsets our efforts by the use of his cheapest and most useful asset – mass manpower.

That lesson had to be re-learned in Vietnam at far greater cost.

Although the introduction of surface-to-air missiles brought a step change in the Soviet defense technology supplied to North Vietnam, the majority of damage to US aircraft still came from essentially the same AAA used in North Korea. Also, the increasing sophistication and greater structural density of Vietnam-era aircraft meant that simple weapons could more easily bring down a jet loaded with complex electronics and systems with a few hits from small-bore guns.

The simplicity of the Panther, with low internal volumetric density, was an advantage in that respect. Former VF-111 F9F-2 pilot Adm James Holloway recalled bringing his aircraft home after hits by a 40mm gun that took off a tiptank and part of the wing and a 20mm shell that broke off the starboard horizontal stabilizer. Eight other pilots survived 40mm hits whilst flying Panthers.

There were long-term benefits for the US forces from the Korean experience. The appearance of MiG-15s in Manchuria, and their obvious superiority over current US Navy fighters (despite some aerial successes by Panther pilots), accelerated the acquisition of the first swept-wing naval fighter. The US Navy had already ordered the McDonnell F3H-1 Demon, but crippling engine problems caused delays and eventual cancellation. Grumman quickly redesigned the F9F-5 with swept wings as the F9F-6, introducing a series of Cougar fighters that entered service in November 1952, just missed the Korean War, and went on to equip 37 US Navy squadrons. Two-seat F9F-8T trainer versions of the Cougar were the mainstay of Naval Air Training Command until February 1974. A few F9F-8Ts flew with the US Marine Corps in Vietnam as tactical air control aircraft until 1966.

The US Navy also began to develop a new generation of fighters that would include the delta Douglas F4D Skyray, the supersonic Vought F8U Crusader, and ultimately the Mach II McDonnel F4H-1 Phantom II, which first flew within five years of the end of the Korean War.

In 1950 the US Navy had 15 active aircraft carriers, with this number rising to 34 by war's end, and with larger and more advanced vessels planned. The conflict in Korea had shown beyond doubt that a powerful carrier force was essential in the areas of the world where land bases were unavailable. For the UN troops holed up in the Pusan perimeter, naval air power undoubtedly saved them from disaster.